Adventure Guide to Trinidad & Tobago

Kathleen O'Donnell & S. Harry Pefkaros

HUNTER
PUBLISHING

Hunter Publishing, Inc.
300 Raritan Center Parkway
Edison NJ 08818, USA
Tel (908) 225 1900
Fax (908) 417 0482

ISBN 1-55650-744-5

Maps by authors, unless indicated otherwise.

Cover photo by George Schaub. Provided by Leo de Wys, Inc.

About The Authors

Jewelry designers by profession and travelers by desire, Harry and Kathleen travel each year when their fine silver business, KRIKA, quiets down for the season. Even before their marriage, each traveled extensively. Harry is most familiar with Europe, the Middle East, and the Caribbean, while Kathleen's interests have taken her south of the border to Latin America and South America. With their primary residence in Taxco, Mexico, Harry and Kathleen spend part of their year working in the United States and a few months in Trinidad and Tobago. Together, they have covered many miles in and out of the States and they write from this broad base of experience.

Acknowledgements

We want to thank our friends in Trinidad, Louis and Gerry Johnston, whose friendship led us to a much better understanding of their diverse and wonder-filled country, and David and Hilary Montgomery for always surprising us with their anecdotes about Trinidad and Tobago. Thanks also go to the engaging Dr. Jesma McFarland of the Chaguaramas Development Authority, to Anne Farfan of the Yacht Services Association, and especially to Jack Dausend, Publisher of the Yachting Directory, to the Directors of TIDCO in both Trinidad and Tobago, and to the Tourism Development Authority in Tobago.

It is impossible to thank personally all those whose generosity made this book a reality. People shared their insights and information, and advised us along the way. We are grateful to them all. We would like to thank Kim André and Michael Hunter of Hunter Publishing for their faith in this project.

Author's Foreword

We decided to visit Tobago after reading a short National Geographic magazine article on the island. We were so impressed that we were back within a month to write this guide.

The guide written, we looked for a publisher. Hunter Publishing said yes, if we would include Trinidad. We returned to explore

Trinidad, planning to make it short and sweet and be off to Tobago to update the book and enjoy ourselves.

As it turned out, Trinidad intrigued us – Carnival events, nature preserves, untraveled roads, wild ocean beaches, and kindness all around. We rewrote the original manuscript and hope that we've done justice to this marvelous country. In so small a place, there is much to enjoy.

Our aim is to give you the best information to make your visit as informed and enjoyable as possible. We have listed a wide range of accommodations, restaurants, beaches, and things to do, but have also tried to give you a sense of how wonderful this twin island country is. The people are open and friendly, the beaches beautiful, and the land enchanting. As the rumor goes, Robinson Crusoe washed up in Tobago and found his tropical paradise. It's still there.

We researched this book carefully to bring you the best of what we found, but no place is unchanging. We welcome your comments for future editions. Please write to us at:

Kathleen O'Donnell and S. Harry Pefkaros
Adventure Guide to Trinidad & Tobago
c/o Hunter Publishing, Inc.
300 Raritan Center Parkway
Edison, NJ 08818

The swing at Maracas Beach

Contents

Maps

Introduction

Why Visit Trinidad & Tobago?

T & T is a country of twin islands, but they are fraternal rather than identical. The familial relationship is there in culture and music, but each has grown in different and special ways. Tobago is Caribbean; Trinidad is South American. Tobago was largely agricultural and is still rural in character. Trinidad's heart and soul have been affected by the wide variety of people who settled there, by a lush jungle in the north and swamps and savannah in the south, and by almost a hundred years of modern industrial development. Together they are a fascinating country with an interesting history, wonderful people, many places to see, and things to do.

Trinidad

Many people visit Tobago and don't take the opportunity of seeing Trinidad. Probably equal numbers visit Trinidad for Carnival and fail to visit neighboring Tobago. There's just no excuse. The two islands are quickly connected by short flights or longer ferry rides and each has its very distinct attractions.

For such a small island, Trinidad offers two almost polar opposite attractions. On the one hand, Trinidad is cosmopolitan. The capital city, Port of Spain, boasts one of the best zoos in the Caribbean and one of the oldest botanical gardens. It has nightclubs and chic restaurants and an air of hustle and bustle that is native to an urban environment. It is also home to one of the biggest parties in the world – Carnival, a spectacular event attracting visitors from all over the world. There is pan music and calypso competitions, parades of fabulously costumed revelers, and dancing in the streets. Officially lasting only a few days, events leading up to the Carnival crescendo start at the beginning of the New Year. It is the best known reason to visit the island and should not be missed.

Less well-known are the wonders of Trinidad's natural environment. Within a short drive from the city you'll find huge mangrove swamps, mountainous jungle rainforests, deserted windswept beaches, two outstanding bird preserves, a pitch lake, island caves, giant iguanas, and a wealth of micro-climates with an enormous variety of plant and animal life. The list goes on and on. Trinidad is a remarkable place.

And don't forget the people of Trinidad. You will find yourself in a true melting pot. Cultures and races have mixed and remixed through the years so that a person's character has finally become more important than his color. Trinidadians are well-educated, politically informed, and sophisticated. Just as important, they are kind, helpful, and open-minded. Wherever you go, you will be treated well.

Trinidad allows you to step into a world where everybody works hard at getting along, and maybe that is its most special quality.

Tobago

Like so many Caribbean islands, Tobago offers an exquisite environment, but it has other major advantages. Although relatively undeveloped for tourism, there are a few resort-style hotels on the island (none is more than three stories high) and there are numerous small hotels and guest houses. Poised between the quiet life of local people and developing tourism, Tobago is still a very friendly and safe island. There are beautiful beaches, of course, but Tobago offers much, much more. It is a birdwatcher's paradise; for nature lovers, it has the oldest national park in this hemisphere; underwater explorers can dive some of the clearest waters in the Caribbean.

Tobago is a wonderful destination for anyone wishing a true Caribbean getaway. It is very relaxed, with sunning and swimming its major attractions. Watersports are available, but they are all low key – snorkeling, diving, deep-sea fishing. There are currently no jet skis or parachute flights on the island and we hope it stays that way. In short, you'll find yourself wishing a part of Tobago could be yours forever.

With assistance and encouragement from the government, however, Tobago is beginning to make its mark on the world of tourism. T & T has an advantage in being late to explore economic development through tourism. It has the rest of the Caribbean to study and learn from. There is a saying in Tobago, an unwritten law, that buildings may not be taller than a palm tree. That law is now being made official and hotels will not be more than three stories anywhere on the island. Attention too is being paid to the delicate ecosystem and fragile nature of the land. While the number of hotel rooms is planned to double, sites are being carefully selected to avoid damaging the very thing that makes the island special, its beautiful environment and clean waters.

As development continues, there is much discussion of what the future will bring. For now, Tobago is a delightful and welcoming destination.

Coastline, Plymouth

Who Else Is Visiting T & T?

The majority of visitors to the islands right now are British, Scandinavian, and German. Americans have long known of the birdwatching opportunities in Trinidad, but only recently are they discovering Tobago.

The People & Their Culture

When visiting Trinidad and Tobago, remember that Tobago, especially, is still an island of villages and small-town friendliness. We got a ride from a farmer one day and as we rode along he talked of the strong village ties in Tobago. Village elders still try to keep everyone on the straight and narrow; there are fewer social problems in Tobago than in nearby more urban Trinidad.

Tobagonians are accepting of visitors and seem to have unending patience with the interruptions in their daily lives caused by tourists. While open minded, the islanders are not sophisticated. Visitors, thoughtlessly sometimes, behave in ways that ignore local customs. Over time, this will only cause friction between the island's people and its visitors. As a tourist, you should pay a little more attention to dress than you may back home. Bathing suits belong only on the beach. Bring a wrap or shorts to throw on when you're leaving the beach and everyone will be more comfortable. Sunbathing also belongs only on the beach or at the pool.

Whether man or woman, remember you're the equivalent of a "city slicker" to just about anyone on the island. Your presence can impress and distort local values on a short-term basis that may have long-term consequences when you leave. As a nation of travelers, we have become more sensitive to taking care of the natural environments we explore. We need to take equal care with the people we encounter.

Tobagonians are deeply religious and, though it may not be immediately evident, they are more straight-laced than you would expect. A local (male or female) who becomes involved with a foreigner will have problems fitting in when the visitor leaves. Be careful not to destroy what you came to see and enjoy.

Language

Although the language of both Trinidad and Tobago is English, it can sound like another language entirely. Here are some local words you might find interesting. "Lime" is to spend time talking and hanging out with friends. You'll see lots of fellows liming during the hotter parts of the day as you drive around the islands; work is done in the cooler morning and evening. "Free up" is to relax and let go of your inhibitions. A "trace" is a road or lane. Calabash houses are the old-style gingerbread houses you'll see as you drive about the islands.

You will please many a person in T & T if you use more formal greetings, such as good morning, good afternoon, and good evening. The informal American greeting, "Hello, how are you?" doesn't seem to do the trick. You'll also hear "good night" used as a greeting, rather than something to say when leaving for the evening.

Geography

The Republic of Trinidad and Tobago is the most southerly Caribbean country. Lying just off the coast of Venezuela, Trinidad is seven miles from the mainland and Tobago another 21. It is believed that these islands broke from the mainland and share many geologic features with Venezuela, unlike many other Caribbean islands, which are of volcanic or coral origin. Visible from one to the other because of their relatively high ridges – 1,860 feet in Tobago and 3,085 in Trinidad – the two islands, though similar in topography, are worlds apart in character.

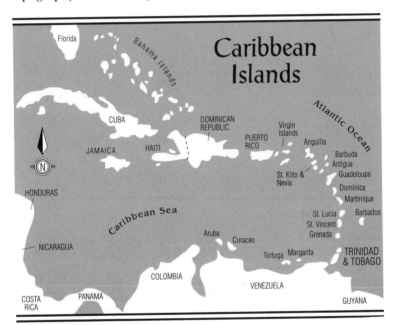

Trinidad In A Nutshell

Physical Description

Trinidad is a fascinating mix of lands and micro-climates in a very tiny package. The island is only about the size of Rhode Island. Combined with its twin, Tobago, it reaches only the size of Delaware.

Roughly a wide rectangle, Trinidad is 50 miles long and 37 miles wide.

The 3,000-foot **Northern Range** runs across the northern coastal edge of Trinidad. Covered in tropical rainforest, the mountain leads down to the sea and provides a dramatic backdrop. On the inland side of the mountain from Port of Spain across to Arima is a strip of mixed commercial and residential development.

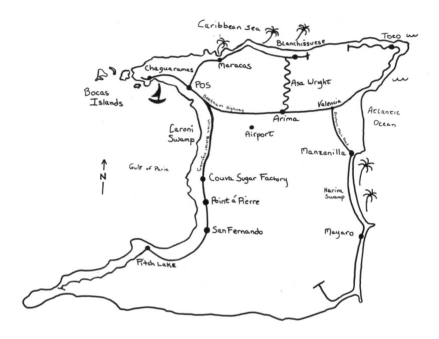

The central area of the island is more level than the north, but is still favored with rolling hills. This central area is also home to mixed development – agriculture, small towns, and manufacturing.

The west coast is less attractive (from a tourist's point of view) than other areas of the country, except in the northwest. The central west coast is home to one of the country's major swamps – the **Caroni**. With dense mangrove, this brackish swamp is the roosting home to thousands of scarlet ibis, the national bird of T & T. Just south of the swamp there is congested residential development, sugarcane agriculture, and the petrochemical industry. Surprisingly, it's also home to **Pointe-à-Pierre**, a wildfowl preserve. Further south is **San Fernando**, the country's second largest city. South of the city is the **Oropuche Swamp** and a pitch lake (one of the only reasons to drive this far on this coast).

Selecting A Hotel Location

Port of Spain & Surrounding Area

Port of Spain is a bustling center of activity by day. By night, most areas of the city are extremely quiet, except around Carnival time. The city streets are organized on a grid system. Were it not for the one-way streets, it would be extremely easy to negotiate. Once you get the hang of which street heads north and which goes south, it is very simple. The city is not large and much of it has a residential character, with offices located in old homes. Port of Spain sits between the ocean and dock area on the south, where the highway has been constructed, and **Queen's Park Savannah** on the north. The Savannah is a very large city park, but it is not remarkable in itself. Surrounding the park, however, you'll find many of the city's key attractions – the magnificent seven, the **Emperor Valley Zoo**, and the **Botanical Garden**. Just past the Savannah you'll find yourself in the suburbs – **Maraval, St. Ann's**, and **Cascade**, to name a few. All in all, the city is small and very manageable on foot or by car.

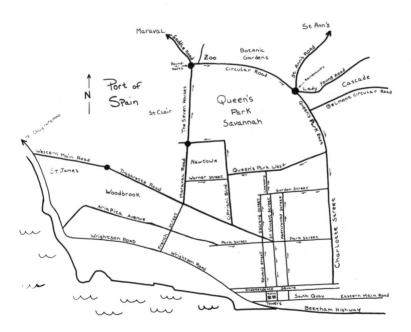

Blanchisseuse

Blanchisseuse is a small fishing village on the sloping northeast coast. It is sandwiched closely between rainforest at its back and the ocean at its feet. It is as quiet as it is beautiful. You will find a few guest houses and restaurants. Trails into the forest abound and Blanchisseuse also offers access to **Paria Waterfall**, a short hike away.

Chaguaramas & the Bocas Islands

These islands lie in the northwestern corner of Trinidad. Called the Dragon's Mouth (Boca in Spanish), with islands as teeth, this small group leads to and protects the Gulf of Paria. Lying between Venezuela and the coast of Trinidad, this sheltered harbor area is being extensively developed for yachts. Chaguaramas, on the mainland, and the Bocas Islands are rich in history and offer many chances to explore the natural environment. Each of the islands has unique attractions – **Gasparee's caves, Chacachacare's leper hospital, salt pond**, and **giant iguanas**, and **Centipede Island's centipedes**. Good swimming beaches can be found on the islands, but stretches of sand are less accessible on the mainland. We have listed one hotel in this area, **The Bight**.

Toco & the Northeast

In the northeastern corner with Toco at the point, you'll find exuberant rainforest and wild beaches. Almost everyone carries a machete; it is a very necessary tool. The waters are primarily for surfing, but you will find a few spots for swimming. The northeast coast is not at all developed for visitors.

Manzanilla & Mayaro, the East Coast

The east coast is largely undeveloped, although there are some small towns. One of the major sights here is the **Nariva Swamp,** about half-way down the coast. The Nariva is quite large, like the Caroni, but it is a fresh-water mangrove swamp and home to monkeys, caiman, and all sorts of other wildlife. The east coast boasts coconut farms and miles of windswept empty beaches. The only town of substantial size on this coast is **Mayaro**, where we discovered a hotel.

Note: Remember that Trinidad is small. From any location, you can drive to the furthest point in two hours or less. It is not developed for tourism; most of the hotel and restaurant services are congregated in and around the capital city of Port of Spain. We'd recommend staying in or around the city. For a beach location, try a few days in Blanchisseuse. Birdwatchers will also want to consider Asa Wright and the Mount St. Benedict guest house.

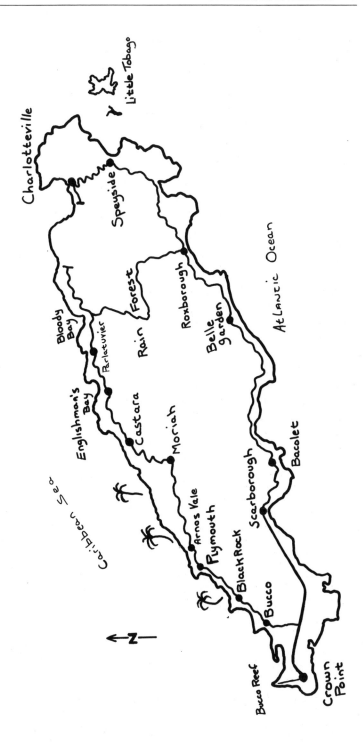

Tobago In A Nutshell

Physical Description

Tobago is small, but geographically diverse. No doubt, you'll find an area that is especially appealing to you.

The island is oval-shaped and just 26 miles long by nine miles wide. Tobago runs from **Crown Point** in the northwest to **Charlotteville** in the northeast on the Caribbean side. On the Atlantic side it runs from **Scarborough** in the southwest to **Speyside** in the southeast. Most of the island's development is on the western end. Down the middle of the island there's a mountain ridge with the hemisphere's oldest forest preserve and very little settlement.

Selecting A Hotel Location

Mid-Caribbean Coast Area – Buccoo, Mt. Irvine, Black Rock, Plymouth & Arnos Vale

These towns are home to the island's resort hotels, vacation homes, and residential areas. It is rural in character now, but there is a lot of development going on and more planned for the future. As you would expect, some of the best beaches on the island are in this area. We didn't find many mid-range hotels and there is almost nothing reasonably-priced or inexpensive on the water. There are a few independent (non-hotel) restaurants and more being built. Arnos Vale is especially attractive, with its rolling hills and peaceful environment.

Crown Point

Home to the airport, Crown Point has lots of small hotels and guest houses. Most of the hotels have fewer than 40 rooms, but there is one new full-service resort-style hotel with over 100 units, named **Coco Reef**. There are lots of open fields with grazing cows, sheep, and goats so it has a very relaxed feel to it. From the porch of our hotel, we just recently saw a calf born, which was a unique experience for us both. Crown Point is primarily a visitors' section of the island, where people come from abroad and from neighbouring Trinidad. There is a holiday feel to the area, with lots of opportunities to meet locals, have a meal out, enjoy Store Bay Beach or Pigeon Point Beach, and all without getting in a car. Coco Reef opened this year, but it hasn't changed the delightfully informal and friendly character of Crown Point.

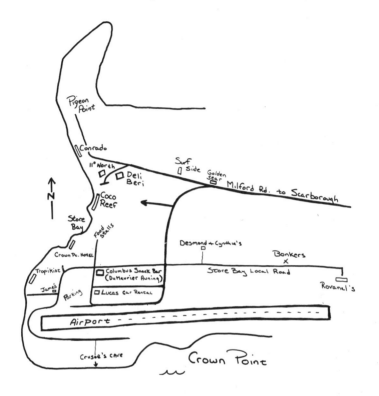

Scarborough

This is the small, bustling, commercial capital of the island and there's not much reason to visit except for the lively food market held on Saturday morning. There are a few other sights to see in Scarborough, but the town itself doesn't offer much. Just outside of Scarborough you'll find Bacolet.

Bacolet

Just to the east of Scarborough, on the Atlantic coast, Bacolet was *the* place to go on the island in times past. There is a lovely coast road offering spectacular views and a good chance to see a few of the old-style gingerbread houses. There's a nice beach (where The Beatles once frolicked), some good restaurants, and one of our favorite hotels – **The Old Donkey Cart.**

Atlantic Coast – Richmond, Roxborough, Delaford

These towns are not developed for tourism and progress will probably be a long time coming. There are primitive accommodations and private homes where you probably could find a room, but, with the exception of the idyllic **Richmond Great House**, there's not much here. It's an interesting part of the island to explore, though, and it's along this coast that you'll find the **Argyle Waterfall** and the **Hillsborough Reservoir**. If you are a birdwatcher, the outskirts of Roxborough are a treasure trove. King's Bay Beach is certainly worth a stop.

Speyside, Charlotteville & Parlatuvier

These towns are at the eastern end of the island. They all have a quiet, remote charm. Speyside is the most lively; Charlotteville and Parlatuvier are almost village-like. Speyside has good hotels and opportunities for finding inexpensive rooms in private homes. The places to stay will easily meet the needs of resort folks or those on a budget, but there's not much in between.

Speyside is certainly the best destination for experienced divers, though more remote Charlotteville also has dive facilities, some near-perfect beaches, and a few accommodations.

If you are looking for an extremely quiet spot, any of these will do. Parlatuvier is my personal favorite; the bay is a perfect shape and absolutely beautiful. Unfortunately, in the past year a concrete fishing wharf was built in the middle of the bay, marring its pristine sands. Parlatuvier has one small, budget hotel.

Government

Organization

The President of T & T is elected Head of State by Parliament. Executive power, however, is held by the popularly elected Prime Minister and his Cabinet. Legislative power resides in the two houses of Parliament – the popularly elected 36-member House of Representatives and the appointed 31-member Senate. Tobago was recently granted more of a voice in its local affairs through a 12-member House of Assembly.

The current Prime Minister is **Basdeo Panday**. He is the first person of Indian heritage to hold that office.

History

The Red House (Parliament) at Woodford Square

T & T gained political independence from Britain in 1962. Since that time it has held elections every five years; powers of government have peaceably transferred with each new ruling party. Because of its history as a Crown Colony, it has less political experience than Britain's other colonies in the Caribbean, most of which enjoyed local political control. They developed political skills, becoming progressively more adept in managing the plurality that makes a democratic process. Crown Colony status for Trinidad meant that its government was appointed by the Crown. Until 1925, the islanders themselves were largely excluded from the political process.

Evidently, their relative lack of experience in the political process did not greatly impede the development of political sophistication.

Trinidad has no army.

Economy

Trinidad and Tobago differ in their history and in their economic development. Tobago is decidedly rural, relying on agriculture, fishing, civil service employment and, more recently, tourism. Trinidad, while having a significant agricultural sector, has diversified manufacturing and a petroleum products industry that developed early in the 20th century.

While current oil reserves might not provide a rosy economic future for the country, natural gas and methanol could save the day.

The BC Sugar Factory

Black Gold

Worldwide oil prices in the 1970's created a financial boon for T & T. Money was suddenly available for major infrastructure expenditures and ambitious projects were undertaken. Unfortunately, with the contraction of oil industry prices in the late 1970's, T & T found itself in a financial squeeze. Like many smaller oil-producing countries, it had greatly over-extended public spending on development projects based on a widely accepted prediction of continued high oil prices. An economic crisis was averted, but there were severe cutbacks in public spending by the late 1980's and even into the 90's. These cutbacks sent waves of recession throughout the economy. With World Bank and IMF involvement, changes in economic policy have been implemented, including a loosening of restraint on foreign investment. The development of a tourism sector in the economy is also a part of these policy changes. Until then, tourism in T & T had never been a significant portion of the economy; it was not perceived as necessary or potentially beneficial.

Tourism

While tourism is a major income-producing sector for many smaller Caribbean countries, it remains to be seen if the industry will appreciably improve or even maintain a desirable standard of living here. Given that T & T is seeking foreign investment, the top economic tier in the tourism industry may not end up being native at all. Extreme care must be taken to ensure that tourism dollars coming into the country do not drain out just as quickly. The lack of tourism capital is a significant problem, especially for small countries that don't have the capacity to produce tourism associated goods – wines and liquors, gourmet foods, TVs, rental cars, etc.

Other Influences

One economic sector with which we have first-hand knowledge is the **yachting industry**. With changing attitudes toward tourism and an especially bad hurricane season in 1995, development of a sophisticated yacht services sector in Chaguaramas is moving rapidly. Only a handful of foreign yachts were in harbor in 1990. By 1995 over 2,500 boats were tied up there. Growth has been phenomenal. Jobs created in this sector are skilled and technical rather than service oriented – a healthy sign.

For an accurate picture of any country's economy you can't rely solely on data. With unjaundiced eyes and an open mind, it must be said that one of the more evident features of the economy is the lack of significant poverty. The extremes of wealth and poverty so prevalent in much of the Caribbean do not exist in T & T. There is a large, well-educated, sophisticated middle class. Although there are areas of the islands where development has failed to improve the standard of living, people do not appear to be in severe need.

When compared to the aging population of the United States, T & T's population is young; almost 30% is under the age of 15. Like the baby boomers in the US, this group will have a significant impact on the country. The government will have to successfully address the education and employment needs of this portion of society if it is to continue improving the standard of living for all its people.

All in all, T & T is an impressive country. While there are tensions among ethnic, and economic groups, there is an upbeat forward movement. They have a wonderful social mechanism for erasing barriers at least once a year when they join together in a national celebration – Carnival.

History

The Republic of Trinidad and Tobago shares much history with other Caribbean countries. That history has determined what it is today – its problems, its culture, and its orientation in the modern world. Understanding some of the historical antecedents of present day T & T will give a richness to your experience of the country, patience with its flaws, and admiration for its achievements.

While each country in the Caribbean shares a lot with its neighbors, each also has unique colonial heritage. Trinidad's experience of colonialism differed remarkably from that of the US, for instance. Britain's control of the American colonies was neither as extensive nor as long lasting as its domination in the Caribbean. The Caribbean was home to relatively few European settlers, there was a large slave/indentured population, economic isolation and dependency, racial divisiveness, and rivalry among all the colonial islands.

The Caribbean's place in history is not wholly unique. The way it was developed and exploited was the rule of the day. Its experience in history was an extension of existing European political, social and cultural patterns. What's most interesting in reviewing the history of Trinidad and Tobago are the ways in which historical antecedents set in motion modern historical developments and helped to define its character in the world of nations.

Trinidad In The 16th-18th Centuries

Columbus discovered Trinidad and claimed it for Spain in 1498. The island at that time was inhabited by Amerindians. It is assumed that both the **Arawak Indians** and probably also the **Caribs** shared the island in an agriculturally based economy. Nearby Tobago was apparently sighted by Columbus, but not claimed.

For a few hundred years, Trinidad was largely ignored by the Spanish, but was viewed as a land open to exploitation. Gold and removable resources were the main aim in Spain's control of the island, not residential colonial development. During this time, of course, the island's Amerindian inhabitants were also seen as a resource and few survived the experience.

Spanish control of the island continued for 300 years, though little progress was made toward the development of a colonial settlement until the latter part of the third century. During that time the Spanish themselves were in conflict about the real goals of colonization. A policy of exploitation and subjugation certainly had its adherents, but there were other voices being raised. Within the Spanish hierarchy there were those who argued for religious conversion and better treatment of native peoples and slaves. These voices were not strong enough, but probably did have a mild restraining influence.

Unlike the more lucrative Spanish incursions into South America, the occupation of Trinidad produced too little economic return for it to receive much attention from the Spanish crown. There were a few agricultural settlers, but the island showed little economic promise until 1718, when cocoa farming brought the island some prosperity. With a crop failure in 1733, Trinidad returned to its position of relative unimportance.

In 1772 Trinidad's total population was under 800, made up by a little over 300 Spanish settlers and a little over 400 Amerindians. In the mid-1770's, the Spanish opened Trinidad to Catholic non-Spanish immigration under the Decree of Population. Both whites and non-whites were enticed to immigrate with monetary benefits in land grants, tax reductions, and export rights. Whites were granted land parcels twice as large as non-whites. Most of the immigrants were French, coming from neighboring islands. Oddly enough, the enticements of the 18th century are much like incentives to foreign investors today – and they were successful.

By 1797, the population had grown to over 16,000 – whites now numbered about 2,100, free Africans about 4,500, and slaves about 10,000. Trinidad was finally developing. It was coincidentally increasing its risk of invasion from without and rebellion from within by free Africans and slaves.

It was not until 1797 that the **British** took Trinidad from the Spanish. In so doing, they were taking on a colony dominated by French culture, administered under Spanish law, and with a large population of Africans, one third of whom were free. Britain had to find the means to ensure Trinidad's economic development, to put the stamp of British culture on an island with few English settlers, and to organize a legal and political structure.

Trinidad's economic future posed some tricky problems. The land had never been heavily used for sugarcane agriculture, as was the case in so many other British colonies. Realizing Trinidad's potential as a competitor, these other colonies strongly opposed any program for the importation of slave labor to Trinidad. Without slave labor, the rich agricultural lands could not be fully exploited and Trinidad would not become a successful competitor. Along with opposition to slavery from other self-interested colonies, Britain's own social reformers were finally succeeding in turning public opinion against the practice. Under these pressures, Britain made it unlawful for agricultural slaves to be imported to Trinidad.

In taking over administration of Trinidad, Britain had an island where British landowners were a relatively small part of the population. Strong French and Spanish influences and the large population of free people of color made it a complex situation. Still, the island had to be administered and in a manner consistent with British interests.

Other British West Indies colonies were constitutionally organized and, to a large degree, self-governing. They might have provided a model for Trinidad, but there were differences. People of color owned a large percentage of the land in Trinidad. In most cases, these people would have enjoyed the right to vote in an organized constitutional government, but this was a group with whom Britain had little experience and granting a self-governing constitution might have led to problems. An alternative was needed and a solution was found.

Trinidad was given the unique status of **Crown Colony**, meaning that all significant decisions were left to the British Government. In establishing this administrative structure, Britain denied the entire population the right to vote and have political control. Few islanders were British and the denial of political rights did not arouse much opposition. Any political voice from landowners was effectively silenced.

Crown Colony status remained in Trinidad until 1925 with few important changes.

Tobago In The 17th & 18th Centuries

Unlike Trinidad, Tobago was ignored by the colony collectors until early in the 17th century. First claimed by the British in 1626, it was later claimed so many times by so many governments that it more than made up for its late start. In 1646 Tobago was claimed by the French and by Holland. Even Latvia staked a claim in 1664, based on a land grant from the English king. While claimed by one and all, Tobago was never settled or defended as a proper colony. Despite that, no one was willing to let go of it permanently.

Even the Spanish became involved. Though not staking a claim to the island, they feared the potential consequences if a coalition of Amerindians from Trinidad and Tobago were to develop. In 1636, the Spanish invaded Tobago. They succeeded in destroying its fortifications and in taking the islanders' store of ammunitions.

In 1749 England and France agreed that Tobago and a few other islands in the area would be neutral. Both controllers left the region, but it wasn't long before England, Holland, and France returned to fight over the island again.

Prospects for development in Tobago did not materialize until 1781, when the French took the island from the British. The French introduced financial incentives to lure immigrants from other islands. Between 1771 and 1791, the island's population grew from just over 5,000 to over 15,000; slaves constituted 14,000 of this total, a startling 94% of the population. By 1796 the island had reverted to the English and sugar production dominated the economy.

Slavery formed the basis for the economies throughout the West Indies in the 18th century, but this was not free of risk and Tobago endured uprisings in 1770 and 1798. Of all the Caribbean islands, only a few were largely settled by immigrant European small farmers, who opposed the slave economies primarily for economic reasons. Opposition based more on humanitarian concerns came from the home countries.

Amidst the battle for possession and economic supremacy no West Indian island wanted to see benefits accrue to another that might make it a successful rival. This competition, which began in the colonial era, continues as a legacy of colonialism and may interfere even today in developing unity among the West Indies countries.

This pattern of claims and counter-claims, small invasions and counter-invasions continued in Tobago until 1803, when the British took over the island from the French for the last time.

Tobago In The 19th Century

In 1834, at the time of **Emancipation**, Tobago was already in economic trouble and, despite all efforts, its financial decline continued throughout the 19th century. The metaire system was introduced as one means of sustaining the economy. Under this system, workers were not paid for their labor, but rather shared in the landowners' profits. This meant that everyone was highly invested in the success of the crops, which guaranteed a degree of social unity and stability. Despite even this system, Tobago's economy declined further.

Politically, however, Tobago had an advantage over the nearby Crown Colony of Trinidad. Tobago had its own representative government. In the first part of the 19th century, Tobago and the British government had clashed repeatedly over Britain's increasingly charitable attitude toward slavery.

In 1833, Britain brought Tobago, Grenada, and St. Vincent under the rule of the Governor of Barbados in an attempt to reduce the cost of governing these small islands. Little changed. Tension between Tobago and Britain continued, with planters refusing to give up control or grant rights to other islanders. In 1876, in the town of Roxborough, this pressure erupted in what was called the Belmanna riots.

Although Tobago had been in a loose political association with other islands since 1833, when Barbados separated from that union in 1885, Tobago made clear its interest in a future association with Trinidad. Britain was not averse to a union of Trinidad and Tobago and subsequently offered Tobagonians two options. First, Tobago and Trinidad could be joined under one government in Trinidad or, second, Tobago might be annexed, but retain its own treasury and a subordinate legislature. Of course, Tobago was more interested in the latter, especially where it related to their rights to collect taxes and expend funds.

Trinidad had nothing to gain from a closer association with bedraggled Tobago, but it was not given a choice. So Tobago and Trinidad were politically associated, but Tobago retained its rights over internal fiscal affairs. As was their political habit, Tobagonians argued for the rights to further fiscal independence in this loose union. In response, Britain decided to bring the two islands closer together, rather than see the existing relationship fall apart. In 1898, Tobago and Trinidad were officially merged – financially and politically.

Acreage in Tobago had been grossly overestimated and was sold in Britain to people who never saw the land and never profited from it. Sometimes the same plots were sold a few times over. Anyone that could throw away their money on an investment in Tobago obviously had cash to burn. A popular 19th-century British saying was "as wealthy as a Tobago landowner."

Trinidad In The 19th Century

With the political and administrative problems solved, Britain addressed Trinidad's economic future. The importation of agricultural slaves had been outlawed, and Trinidad had to find other sources of affordable labor. Efforts to attract significant numbers of European settlers and colonists from other islands were unsuccessful. Never giving up, however, they tapped an entirely new labor pool. Indentured laborers from China were recruited and in the early 1800's over 300 Chinese workers arrived. Unfortunately, only men were recruited. Without families and largely unaccepted by other islanders, the men were not willing to stay.

To sustain the labor pool, many landowners found illegal ways of obtaining slaves and, despite labor shortages during this period, Trinidad progressed in its agricultural development, producing sugar, cotton, coffee, and cocoa, an especially prized crop at that time.

In the years preceding the abolition of slavery, changing laws increasingly provided protection to the people forced into this degraded economic system of human ownership. But changing laws was not enough. Finally with the Emancipation Bill of 1834, slavery was abolished altogether. Under this act, slaves were freed, but slave owners were also compensated for their losses. Compensation granted to slave owners in Trinidad was higher than in other West Indies islands because of the slaves' higher economic worth.

While outright slavery was abolished, slaves were not yet really free. There would be an apprentice period of several years, during which freed slaves were required to work for their former masters at defined hours and wages. This did not sit well with those who now considered themselves free and in time the apprentices went on strike.

Other changes came with Emancipation. Britain had already solved the problem of non-white land ownership and voting rights by creating Trinidad's Crown Colony status. With large numbers of freed persons of color, the issues of land ownership would have to be addressed all over again. And so a move was made to permit only large holdings, ostensibly because large areas of land were necessary to make cane agriculture economically viable. This had secondary benefits. It maintained a non-landholding labor pool dependent on plantation work for income and limited the size of the non-white landholding group.

Emancipation did not cause labor shortage problems in Trinidad, but it made existing shortages more severe. Once again, a new

History

source of labor was drawn upon, this time from India. Between 1845 and 1917, about 145,000 indentured Indian workers were imported to work in the agricultural industry.

Learning from previous recruitment errors, Indian workers would be imported with all their cultural and social requisites. Trinidad would fund the program, including transportation, medical services and paying the cost of policing newcomers during their time on the island. Wages were set low enough to ensure profitability.

The British wrote laws governing everything related to immigrants and indentured workers. Reading them, one can't help but feel it was a whole new form of slavery. Plantation owners were granted protection from their workers. Owners' responsibilities for providing work and remuneration were defined. Workers, as well, were given specific rights and responsibilities. But, while provisions were made for adequate housing and working conditions, they were not enforced. Housing and sanitation facilities were extremely poor and illness was common, resulting in lost work hours. Wages for indentured workers were extremely low relative to other forms of labor on the island. With all the restrictions imposed on indentured workers, their only viable option was passive resistance – slow work, and absences.

Unfortunately, the grossly inadequate living conditions and illness were interpreted as cultural characteristics of the Indians, not as a result of the situation in which they labored. Indentured workers were blamed for the very conditions imposed on them.

Conditions were sufficiently intolerable that a large number of indentured workers opted to return to India when their servitude was completed. By law, return passage was to be paid for by the government. To avoid growing transportation expenses, it was decided to offer small plots of land in exchange for return passage, usually five to 10 acres. This decision was inadvertently one of the better and more lastingly favorable laws passed. It developed a larger pool of non-white landowners, many of whom planted sugarcane. They were successful enough to raise questions within the Crown Colony about the whole idea of a sugar plantation – that it had to be large and that a subclass of poorly paid workers was necessary to its economic success.

In 1897 the sugar industry collapsed throughout the West Indies. Sugar production in the Caribbean couldn't compete in a world market. It faced competition not only from countries with more fertile and more productive land, but Trinidad had also failed to keep up with developments in mechanization that improved yields. Britain's level of concern for her Crown Colony was evidenced in the report produced by its commission sent out to study the problem. They recognized that sugar plantations had failed and recommended that islanders diversify.

Trinidad's Crown Colony status continued to preclude the development of island-based political and economic control. Why Britain held on is not very clear. There could not have been more than sparse economic benefits. Retaining the colony apparently became an end in itself.

T & T In The 20th Century

Trinidad and Tobago entered the 20th century as one country. Not long after, in 1910, oil was discovered in Trinidad. Trinidad went from a Crown Colony of little interest to one of the stars in the colonial system. The new century brought other changes as well. After almost 100 years, the indenture system came to an end. Another change came with the end of WWI, when returning West Indian soldiers brought with them a new perspective of the world, of themselves, of their country, and their political rights. Out of these changes developed a movement for self-government and the creation of the **Trinidad Labor Party.** Demand for political reform began to occur throughout the West Indies.

Voting rights were granted in 1925 under restrictive guidelines and that year saw the first election in Trinidad. Trinidad's first elected officials, along with a group of appointees, acted as advisors to the Governor, who had ultimate control. It was not real political representation, but it was a beginning.

Unfortunately, it was not smooth sailing for the newly-elected officials. The year 1929 brought the sugar industry once again to the brink of bankruptcy, this time due in major part to worldwide over-production and falling prices. Trinidad's cost of production was average, but Britain remained unwilling to commit financial support to Trinidad's sugar exports when it could buy goods cheaper on the open market.

And time moved on. Trinidad's oil industry gave the impression that it was a colony without the problems of other less resource-rich Caribbean colonies, but that picture was far from accurate. A 1937 commission sent to study problems in T & T found an extremely low standard of living very common and recommended new housing and sanitation facilities, which were planned, but never built. People lived in squalor.

The **Commission of 1937** was formed in response to disturbances in Trinidad resulting not only from poverty, but from the absence

History

of mechanisms by which labor could address its grievances. Labor had no legitimate voice and the result was as predictable as it was unfortunate. While sugar and oil production increased, other agricultural products failed and the economic division between oil industry and agricultural workers widened. Slavery and the indenture system had guaranteed at least some rights to workers. With the advent of free labor, all rights were lost. Goodwill of the employer was the last and only resort for the workers.

In 1937 there was what could be called a general strike, sparked by a sit-down strike in the oil fields. It resulted when police attempted to arrest an oil industry labor leader as he addressed the workers. Unrest and frustration was just below the surface and disturbances soon raged across the island.

During WWI, Britain, over the objections of Trinidadians, granted permission for the United States to develop a naval base on the island in return for warships. Chaguaramas was selected as the site and the deal between Britain and the US was accomplished despite protests from even the British Governor of Trinidad and Tobago. The base was built under a 99-year lease agreement and became a long-term contentious issue between the US and Trinidad and Tobago, as well as adding one more strain to its relationship with Britain.

In 1946, Trinidad held its first election with universal suffrage. With little experience in the political process, no party won a majority and little was accomplished toward achieving the goals of reform and independence. It was not until 1956, 10 years later, that a new party coalition called the **People's National Movement** (PNM) won a majority in the elections and became Trinidad and Tobago's first party government. The PNM was led by Dr. Eric Williams, an Oxford educated scholar and politician. Williams was later to be the country's first Prime Minister, taking office in 1962 and holding the position until his death in 1981.

In the next election, in 1961, PNM again won a majority with two thirds of the seats in the general election. Their platform included political education, independence from Britain, morality in public affairs, equal rights for women, and a coalition of all races and religions.

In his book on the history of his country, Williams speaks proudly of the achievements of the PNM which, most significantly, led to full internal self-government. The Republic of Trinidad and Tobago became an independent member of the British Commonwealth on August 31, 1962 and in 1976 became an independent republic with a fully democratic government. After Eric Williams died, the political power he had wielded for so many years was up for grabs.

Other political parties gained strength and in 1986 the **National Alliance for Reconstruction** was voted in over the PNM, bringing Prime Minister Robinson into power.

Beginning in the 1980's T & T underwent serious economic problems following an economic boom in the 1970's. These swings were largely due to the rise and fall in oil prices, as well as ambitious investment in infrastructure. Trinidad is only now recovering.

July of 1990 brought a coup attempt on the government of T & T. The police station in Port of Spain was blown up and politicians, including the Prime Minister, were held hostage. Factions behind the coup were not widely supported in the populace and it was unsuccessful. Normalcy returned shortly after and the government resumed its work. We discussed the coup attempt and its impact on the local residents with friends of ours in Trinidad. Their reaction was much like that of Americans when the Federal building in Oklahoma City was blown up. We were outraged, but we did not fear a collapse of the government.

History

Summary

Trinidad and Tobago appear to be on very solid footing as they enter the 21st century. There is a stable democratic government and an improving economy. Divisiveness does still exist among workers, races, and classes, but it is one of the few countries where color matters less than character, where extremes of rich and poor are not prevalent, where recovery from its colonial past is well underway.

The Old Police Station

Plants & Animals

Trinidad and Tobago provide extraordinary opportunities to explore nature in all its forms. There are over 400 species of birds, over 600 varieties of butterflies, monkeys, armadillos, caiman, lizards, over a hundred species of snakes, and a huge variety of fish and other marine life. All of these find homes in an astonishing variety of natural environments – saltwater and freshwater mangrove swamps, mountain and coastal rainforests, savannahs, coral reefs, deep water caves, freshwater rivers, and city parks. There are over 2,300 varieties of flowering plants, and it seems there are almost as many micro-climates to support them.

Water lilies at the Pitch Lake

Nature in Tobago is more accessible than in Trinidad, where you will need to travel a distance from your hotel to hike or boat through natural preserves. While these opportunities are rugged, they are definitely not at your front door. When you learn that some areas of Trinidad receive up to 120" of rain a year, you can only begin to imagine the possibilities for growth. In Tobago, the terrain is more gentle, less overpoweringly lush. That said, each island has its attractions and neither should be missed.

Trinidad

The national bird of Trinidad is the scarlet ibis. One of the more popular excursions is a visit to the Caroni Swamp, where you will see thousands of scarlet ibis returning to roost for the night. We were told that it is not unusual for birders to add well over a hundred new species to their "life-list" during a short stay in Trinidad.

Unlike many of the forest animals common to both islands, monkeys are seen only in Trinidad. You may see howlers in the Nariva Swamp on the east coast or, oddly enough, at the Pointe-à-Pierre Golf Course on the west coast.

The familiar **armadillo** is called a tatoo in T & T and it is considered tasty food. With its nocturnal habits, you probably won't see one.

The **agouti** resembles a large rodent. This timid animal eats fruits and vegetables and is about the size of a large cat. While normally diurnal, it will become nocturnal if bothered during the day. It has long been hunted for food and commercial farming of the agouti is now being considered in Trinidad.

Snakes are common in Trinidad, and you'll find them in all sizes. There are even a few highly poisonous species – the bushmaster, pit viper, and two varieties of coral snake.

Coming from a temperate climate where reptiles are less prevalent, we were surprised to see the wide variety and common presence of snakes. At the Asa Wright Bird Sanctuary, they have a terrarium with snakes behind the office desk. When we stepped outside to start the tour, a worker came by and laughingly pointed up. We were not 15 feet from the estate house door and only a few feet over our heads was a resting tree snake, all curled up comfortably, taking the sun, patiently waiting for a head on which to drop. If you have a special interest in snakes, talk to Alan Rodriguez, the Grounds Supervisor at Asa Wright. He has a snake collection and is very knowledgeable about the varieties found in Trinidad.

Two of the more common flowering trees found in T & T are the **poui** and the **flamboyant**. In January and February, you'll see the poui tree in bloom all over the islands in drier areas. Its delicate pink or yellow flowers do not stay for long, but make a lovely show while they last. With bright reddish orange flowers, the flamboyant stands out all over the hills. It is commonly planted among cocoa trees.

Plants & Animals

Tobago

While we are not ornithologists, Tobago also seems to be a bird-watcher's heaven, and you don't have to travel far to enjoy our feathered friends. We had continuing bird song and visits from a whole variety of birds, large and small, at all of the hotels we visited. From any window ledge on the island you can create a bird feeding station with a little sugar or a banana. We even made a birdbath for the tinier ones with a bowl of water. It gave us endless joy to see the hummingbirds, canaries, and parakeets dine and bathe.

The **cocrico** is the national bird for Tobago. They are not at all delicate, but can be quite pretty, with a long tail, red feathers under the neck, and a mahogany-brown torso. The cocrico is big, loud and causes lots of trouble in the garden. It can be quite amusing to hear them gossip in the trees.

One of the most interesting animals we found in Tobago was the **twenty-four-hour lizard** or *gommangalala*. This unusual lizard is 10 to 12" long and lives in the trees. It's harmless until molested, when it will drop onto you and stick to your skin for 24 hours. After that it simply falls off. We saw lots of them at Englishman's Bay. Bring some sweet bread to feed them; they are quite friendly.

There are no poisonous snakes in Tobago, but watch for the **coco police,** who live on cocoa trees and guard the chocolate pods.

Tobago, as well as Trinidad, is a nesting home for the extraordinary **leatherback turtle**, the largest species of marine turtle. Weighing over a half-ton, leatherbacks nest on the Caribbean side of the island from March to August. Grafton Beach in Stone Haven Bay and Turtle Beach in Great Courland Bay are good sites to observe the turtles as they arrive to lay their eggs after dark. If you are staying at the Turtle Beach Hotel, the staff will let you know when a turtle is coming. Otherwise, you can take your chances sitting on the beach in the evening (not a bad thing to do in the company of friends). Once eggs are laid, they take about two months to develop. Hatchlings make a dash to the sea, but few survive to return.

Nesting turtles are extremely shy creatures. Their nesting behavior is an instinctual pattern and disturbances can break their routine entirely. They have been known to turn back to the sea before laying their eggs if the beach has been artificially lit. Nonetheless, they are a marvel to see and you can do so without disrupting them. Stay at least 50 feet away, be very quiet, and use no lights. Let your eyes naturally adjust to the darkness; this is the dry season and the night sky will not usually be overcast. As your night vision develops, you'll be able to see well, without disturbing these magnificent creatures.

Cocoa

Throughout Trinidad and in the Roxborough area of Tobago, you'll see shiny rusty-green-leaved small bushy trees. Hanging from many branches and trunks will be yellow, purple, red, and brown pods, each six to eight inches in length. This is chocolate. Or at least, this is its beginning, cocoa.

In Trinidad, the heaviest concentration of cocoa estates may be found in Toco, Paria, and Blanchisseuse, but cocoa seems to be everywhere there is sun and lots of water. You will almost always find the orange flowering flamboyant tree growing among the cocoa.

Cocoa has a long history in T & T. Historically, chocolate was prized and cocoa plantations were highly profitable. Unfortunately, cocoa is trickier to grow than it appears. Crop failures were significant and cocoa became a less fashionable agricultural crop, though it is still produced on a small scale in Trinidad.

Cocoa House on the Lopinot Estate

From my point of view, as a chocolate lover interested in plants, the cocoa is an oddity. The large many colored pods grow right from the main trunk. Where have you seen anything like that? Cocoa grows in dense rainforest and competes successfully with other plants. Yet the cocoa does not often take well to artificial fertilizers. Fallen leaves are left beneath the tree to keep the ground cool, yet the plant grows well in the tropics where cool is just a state of mind.

Plants & Animals

Cocoa pods are harvested from October to March. The pods are picked, split open, and wrapped in banana leaves for four to six days. They are then cleaned of their contents, which is moved to the cocoa house for drying, where it will stay in the sun for six to seven days. An ingenious design, the cocoa house has a movable roof just like a sliding door, only sideways. The cocoa is placed on the floor just under the roof and bakes in the heat. In the evening, the roof slides back into place and keeps the evening dew or rain from wetting the beans.

Once the beans are aged and dried, "dancing the cocoa" will begin. The cocoa beans are given a touch of water or oil and the feet begin to move. Dancing the cocoa makes it shiny and shiny cocoa brings more profit. A good price for dried cocoa beans right now in Trinidad is a little over $1/kilo.

Preparation

Planning Your Trip, A-Z

Banks & Money

The value of the TT dollar floats in the international currency market and the exchange rate varies from time to time. At press time it was running at about $5.80 TT to $1 US for travelers checks exchanged at banks. The exchange rate for US dollars varies. Sometimes US dollars will get you more TT dollars than traveler's checks, at other times, less.

While it is almost always better to use travelers checks for security, you can comfortably pay with US dollars in many places. (Since the exchange rate for dollars usually is less than for travelers checks, your purchases will end up costing a little more – perhaps a few cents per dollar – and for the convenience, it's often worth it.) Hotels will almost always quote prices in US dollars and you can readily pay with travelers checks or credit cards.

Credit cards are welcomed for most major expenses. Always check ahead of time to see which of your cards gives you a more favorable exchange rate. We used two cards while in the islands the first time and were surprised to learn that one gave us a better rate than the other. You can guess which card we used on the next trip. Overseas credit card charges may not appear on your bills immediately.

Exchanging **travelers checks** in Trinidad is most convenient in Port of Spain. There are many banks to choose from and all are open from 8 AM to 2 PM Monday through Thursday, and 8 AM to 12 PM and 3 to 5 PM on Fridays. Generally, there are not long lines and changing money is a quick process. Should you run short of cash, you will find banks in almost all towns.

The most convenient place to exchange travelers checks in Tobago is the **Republic Bank** at Crown Point Airport. It is open from 8 to 11 AM and 12 to 2 PM, Monday through Thursday, and 8 to 12 AM and 3 to 5 PM on Friday; closed on weekends and holidays. There are several other banks in Scarborough and all have similar hours, but parking can be a problem. Hotels will exchange travelers checks for you, but the rate will not be as good as at the bank.

Climate

T & T is relatively close to the equator and could be oppressively hot, but it's not. Tempered by cooling tradewinds, the average year-round temperature in Trinidad is 83° Fahrenheit. In Tobago the daily temperature average is 84°, dropping to 74° at night. The sun is very strong, so you'll need a good sunscreen and should remember to drink lots of water. (Water is safe to drink on the islands, but bottled water is available if you prefer it.) If you have a room with cross ventilation, you'll be able to enjoy the cooling night-time breezes. Forget all about air conditioning; you won't need it.

There are distinct dry and rainy seasons, late winter and spring being drier. Rain sometimes falls during the dry season, January through May, and will come on fast and leave just as quickly, giving just a brief respite from the sun. Trinidad and Tobago differ in annual rainfall and even within these small islands, rainfall differs significantly from place to place. Some areas are lush year round, with an average of 90 inches of rainfall. Other regions are quite dry, such as the grasslands in Tobago. A visit to either island in spring will provide you with lots of green, but not as much as on a rainy season visit.

Crime

Unlike many areas of the world, T & T is not a dangerous place. In fact, it is surprisingly free of crime and unpleasant human interactions. True, it is not as safe as it once was, but what place is? Islanders talk of their once-idyllic island and complain of changes. The fact that you can't leave a camera on the beach anymore while you go for lunch is a sore subject.

While crime is a problem that affects all of us, our awareness of the potential for problems has, in some cases, made us overly cautious. While visiting T & T, take all the precautions you would at home and you should have no problems at all.

- Don't leave your possessions on the beach while you go to lunch.
- Don't leave money and valuables in your hotel room (check them at the desk).
- Don't walk alone in lonely dark areas.
- If someone should pester you with something to sell or for any other reason, make it clear in simple vocal terms that you are not interested and go on with your business.

Overall, we found T & T to be a safe and friendly environment. People were always helpful and kind. Let's hope that visitors to the island don't encourage or invite a change in the islanders' very civilized and generous traditions.

In the event of an emergency – medical or otherwise – do contact your embassy for help.

EMBASSIES

Embassy of the United States
15 Queen's Park West, Port of Spain
☎ 622-6371

High Commission for Canada
Huggins Building, 72-74 South Quay, Port of Spain
☎ 623-7254

High Commission for UK and Northern Ireland
19 St. Clair Ave., St. Clair
☎ 622-2748

Embassy of Germany
7-9 Marli St., Newtowne
☎ 628-1630

Embassy of the Kingdom of the Netherlands
3rd floor, Life of Barbados Building
69-71 Edward St., Port of Spain
☎ 625-1210

Equipment

Bicycles

Tobago: If you ride and have a good mountain bike, you'll love it here. The roads are not in great condition, but with a mountain bike they're no problem. Racing bikes are a little too delicate for this terrain. Riding is a great way to get around, but watch that you drink enough water and use a good sunscreen; the heat can be oppressive. Bikes can be rented on the island for about $7, but if you love yours, bring it. Airlines are now charging about $45 to ship a bike each way from the US to the Caribbean. Air Caribbean does not charge to transfer a bike from Trinidad to Tobago.

Binoculars

T & T: These are wonderful tools for birdwatchers and will increase everybody's enjoyment of the outdoors. You can watch sailboats and fishermen come in to harbor and see the small animals and birds so abundant in T & T.

Snorkel, Masks & Fins

Tobago: These are available for rent on a daily basis for about $7, but it's wonderful to have your own at hand when the mood strikes. The quality of equipment you might own yourself is likely to be superior to what you'll find commonly available for rent.

Cooking Tools

Tobago: If you'll be staying at a hotel or guest house with kitchen facilities, you may want to bring your favorite wooden spoon, a knife sharpener, and a good frying pan.

AUTHORS' PET PEEVE
Lampshades In Tobago

In some of the smaller hotels and guest houses, you'll find bare light bulbs. We always find these horrible looking and impossible to read by. The problem is easily solved if you bring Japanese or Chinese paper lanterns to soften the light and cut the glare.

Cameras & Film

T & T: Above and below the water you'll find a wealth of activity.

Expenses

T & T has a wide variety of hotels, from plush to primitive. One thing it does not have is noticeable friction between visitors and locals. That means you are free to select a hotel and go about the island finding local restaurants and seeing the sights. You need not feel concern that you will run into something unpleasant when you leave your hotel.

So, rent a car, visit the sights, stop for a snack, laze on a deserted beach, and settle in for dinner at a place you find appealing. Be at home.

For all this freedom, you'll find yourself spending less than you would at a full-fledged resort. And, you'll be having more fun. Trinidad and Tobago are bargains by Caribbean standards. With tourism just now developing, there is much competition for your business and bargaining is as worthwhile as it is entertaining.

MINIMUM ESTIMATED DAILY EXPENSES

Average dinner for two	$30 to $60
Mid-range hotel for two	$50 to $125
Car rental and gas	$40/day
Taxi (one ride for two)	$4

Health

If you might be sexually active while in T & T, bring along a good supply of condoms; you don't want to bring home an unattractive souvenir or pass one along yourself.

Bring a supply of prescription medicine you may require.

Watch out for sunburn. The sun in this part of the world will burn you much faster than you think. Bring a good sun block and use it liberally.

If you should have a serious medical problem, try to have it treated in your native country, where you will be more comfortable and familiar with the medical system.

The **Port of Spain General Hospital** is at 169 Charlotte St., right in the downtown area. Hopefully, you will never have to use their phone number, ☎ 623-2951/52/53.

The **Tobago County Hospital** is in Scarborough, ☎ 639-2551.

Planning Your Trip

Holidays & Special Events

While traveling on national holidays can present logistical problems in some countries, this is not the case in T & T. There are a few exceptions. The busiest time of year is during Carnival, when visitors arrive from all over the world to witness or participate in this extravaganza. You will not find a hotel room without prior reservations. If you plan to be in T & T for Carnival, reservations need to made at least six months in advance. Next busiest times are at Christmas and Easter, especially in Tobago, where many Trinidadians spend their holidays. Summer can also present problems, again on Tobago, because it is an ideal family vacation spot.

Other holidays are usually religious in nature. Exact dates are determined late in the year and the holiday itself should not affect your trip. If you have a special interest in one of the holidays listed below, contact the T & T Tourism Department to confirm dates (see below).

HOLIDAYS

New Year's Day	January 1
Carnival 1997	February 10 & 11
Carnival 1998	February 23 & 24

Carnival is not an official holiday, but if this celebration doesn't qualify, I don't know what does.

Good Friday	March 28
Easter	April 3

Easter on Tobago takes on a special flavor, with goat and crab races (enthusiasts actually breed racing goats!) and festivities all over the island. Easter Sunday there's a big party at Buccoo, starting at 10 PM, and continuing till dawn.

Angostura/	
Yachting World Regatta Race Week	May 12-17
Whit Monday	June
Phagwah	To be determined

Hindus celebrate the advent of spring with this holiday which, over time, has developed an almost Carnival atmosphere. This is a holiday celebrated in Trinidad.

Corpus Christi	May 6

This is a special day for Catholics, who plant crops to celebrate.

Labour Day	June 19
Tobago Heritage Festival	July

This is a two-week celebration of the island's village traditions. The festivities include theater, dance, and special foods.

The Great Speedboat Race   July
This is one of the great events of the year, a speedboat race covering 85 miles from Trinidad to Tobago. In 1997, the race will be in its 29th consecutive year.

Emancipation Day   August 1
Independence Day   August 31
Celebrated largely in Trinidad, this day marks independence from Britain.

Eid-ul-Fitr   To be determined
Celebrated by the Muslim population based in Trinidad, the sighting of the new moon marks the beginning of the Islamic New Year – Eid ul Fitr. This day marks the end of the month-long Ramadan fast and is a day of feasting, prayer, donations to the poor, and gifts exchanged between relatives and friends.

Republic Day   September 24
Divali   Oct./Nov.
This is the Hindu festival of lights, honoring the goddess Lakshmi. Devout Hindus place thousands of little earthenware lamps around their homes and temples.

Hosay   Fall
A Muslim religious festival featuring booming tassa drums and colorful processions marking a special time of year in the Muslim calendar, 10 days after the new moon. On one of the days, paraders march through the streets singing and carrying tadjahs, very large and elaborately decorated models of the tombs of Mohammed's grandsons. This celebration is largely restricted to Trinidad.

Pan Jazz Festival   November (3 days)
Christmas Day   December 25
Boxing Day   December 26
Boxing day becomes a great day for anniversaries as it is a tradition to marry on this holiday.

Immigration & Customs

Although travelers have encountered problems clearing customs, we have never experienced any ourselves. Customs and immigration officers seem efficient and professional.

You are allowed to bring a carton of cigarettes and one quart of liquor per person without duty.

The duty-free allowance from T & T is $400, but you might have problems spending that much!

Just Facts

Area

Tobago covers 16 square miles, the size of Martha's Vineyard.
Trinidad covers 1,864 square miles, about the size of Rhode Island.
Together, they are about the size of Delaware.

Population

Tobago: 47,000 (as of 1994)
Trinidad: 1,210,000 (as of 1994)

Electricity

110/220 volts, 60 cycles – good for American and European appliances.

Passport & Visa

All visitors to T & T are required to have valid passports, including US citizens. Visitors from some countries (other than the US) must have visas.

Emergency Numbers

Police: Dial 999
Fire & Ambulance: Dial 990

Time Zone

One hour ahead of EST.

Language

English.

Mailing Address

Republic of Trinidad & Tobago, West Indies. To avoid having your mail go to WI (Wisconsin), it is best to spell out "West Indies."

Area Code

Area code from the US is (809), which you should use like any other area code (dial 1-809, followed by the phone number). Note: This area code may be changing. If you have trouble getting through, check with your long distance company.

What To Pack

Comfortable cool clothing. The islands are very informal. In the evening at resort hotels, women can rely on casual elegant clothing. Long pants may be required for men in the evening. Port of Spain is the only place where dressier, but still informal clothes might be appropriate.

Water Supply

Tap water is drinkable. Bottled water is readily available. We recommend water that has been treated by the reverse osmosis technique; it tastes better.

Departure Tax

The equivalent of $15 US or $75 TT, which must be paid in TT dollars.

Library

The library on Tobago is between the bus station and the mall in Scarborough (☎ 639-3635). There you'll find books on local architecture and culture. The library has an interesting system for book loans, whereby you purchase "pockets," (the card that goes in the back of the book indicating the return date) for just under $1 each. As a temporary member of the library you are allowed two books at a time.

The library is always looking for book donations. Librarian, Miss Johnson, expressed their special need for books in the following areas: environment, sexual harassment, child abuse, teenage coping skills, health related to AIDS, handcrafts (basket making, weaving, flower arranging, tailoring), Caribbean history and popular novels. Any donations that you may make of new or used books will be greatly appreciated. Send books to: Public Libraries (Tobago Branch), Scarborough, Tobago, Republic of Trinidad & Tobago, West Indies.

Maps

Unless you are looking for some very specialized information, tourist maps are adequate for getting around. There just aren't that many roads to choose from on either Trinidad or Tobago.

Planning Your Trip

Newspapers

The *Sunday Newsday* and two dailies – *The Guardian* and *The Express* – are widely available. There are also a number of weeklies – *Punch, Bun, Heat,* and *Mirror* – that provide local gossip, lots of pictures of women in bathing suits, and sensational news.

Telephones

As in the US, coin phone booths in T & T are becoming a rarity. You can buy phone cards in denominations of 20, 60, and 100 TT plus tax at the TSTT company at 18 Park St. in downtown Port of Spain, Trinidad. The TSTT is open from 8 to 4 PM Monday through Friday. Many hotels and guest houses on both islands also sell telephone cards.

Local calls are very reasonable, costing only about 4¢ for 2½ minutes; between Trinidad and Tobago it is 12¢.

The area code to T & T from the United States is 809 (call your long distance company if you have problems getting through as this may be changing). There is no area code between the two islands.

Long distance calls from T & T to the US or UK are least expensive if you use the local TSTT phone card. Numbers that are toll-free in the US can be called from T & T by dialing 880 instead of 800. You will be charged about $1 per minute.

Television

Cable is offered in some hotels, which means you'll get three channels – TNT from the US and two local stations. Satellite TV usually means you'll get an additional six stations.

Tipping, Service Charges & Taxes

There is a relatively new tax in T & T called VAT (Value Added Tax). I've never understood what value gets added, but the tax man gets an extra 10 to 15%. It applies to all of your major expenses while in the country – hotels, restaurants, and car rentals. If you don't see it on a bill, assume it has been included.

Don't confuse VAT with the 10% service charge, which is automatically added to most of your bills in hotels and restaurants. The service charge is collected and divided among staff. If you get particularly good service in a hotel or restaurant, don't hesitate to acknowledge it with an additional gratuity. And don't forget the maid who cleans your room; $2 a day will be genuinely appreciated.

Tourist Information

The following telephone numbers have been set up by the Tourism and Industrial Development Company (TIDCO) in Trinidad to provide you with up-to-date travel information. Some of these numbers are toll-free and, with fingers crossed, all will be working by the time of your visit.

From the UK	☎ 0-500-89-2313
From the US	☎ 1-800-595-1TNT
From Germany	☎ 0-130-81-1618
From Italy	☎ 1-678-70272

TIDCO's internet address is: http://www.tidco.co.tt

There are tourist information offices in both Trinidad and Tobago. The most useful one we found was at the **Piarco Airport** in Trinidad. On all of our visits there, staff were well-informed and anxious to help. When we told them the sort of hotel we were looking for and gave them a price range, they made a few recommendations, answered our questions, and called ahead to make a reservation. There is also a wealth of well-written printed matter on everything you might need.

In Tobago, tourist information services are another matter. Just across the street from the Crown Point Airport, the Tourist Bureau is staffed by people who don't appear to be interested in answering any questions. They will give you a list of B & B's with phone numbers, locations, and prices. There are also names and phone numbers of hotels and tour services posted on the wall but, as a visitor, you won't have a clue where they are or what they're like. There's another tourist office in Scarborough, but it was closed every time we visited.

Don't let the lack of formal tourist information in Tobago discourage you. Anyone you meet on the street is more than willing to impart whatever information he/she has to offer.

Planning Your Trip

Transportation

Airlines

Air Canada, ☎ 800-422-6232, has four daily flights to Miami connecting with BWIA for flights to Port of Spain, Trinidad and Crown Point, Tobago. There are also three weekly nonstop flights to Port of Spain.

Air Caribbean, in Port of Spain (☎ 623-2500), makes the short hop between Trinidad and Tobago. Lasting only 20 minutes, the flight may remind you of what flying used to be. There's leg room, adequate aisle space, it doesn't smell bad, and it runs pretty much on time. We were delighted. They have daily flights from Tobago to Trinidad at 7, 9, 11 AM and 1, 5, 7, and 9 PM. From Trinidad to Tobago, flights leave at 6, 8, 10, and 12 AM and 2, 4, 6, and 8 PM. The cost is just $20 one way.

American Airlines, ☎ 800-624-6262, has one daily nonstop flight from Miami to Port of Spain, Trinidad. They also have one flight leaving from New York with a stop in Miami, but no change of planes. The Port of Spain American Airlines office is at 63-65 Independence. Service is extremely slow.

British Airways, ☎ 800-247-9297, does not fly into T & T, but does fly to Barbados, where you can change to **Liat** (☎ 623-1837) for a flight to Port of Spain, Trinidad or Crown Point, Tobago.

BWIA, ☎ 800-538-2942, offers daily flights from Miami to Port of Spain, Trinidad and flights to Tobago twice a week. From New York, BWIA has daily flights to Port of Spain and a once weekly flight to Tobago. They also have flights to Port of Spain originating in Toronto, connecting with **Air Caribbean** (☎ 623-2500) for the flight to Tobago.

Caledonian Airways, ☎ 800-338-2410. Flights originate in the UK, but schedules vary. Check with them directly for the latest information.

Liat, ☎ 623-1837 (in Port of Spain) is a Caribbean-based airline making the short hops between Caribbean islands.

Ferries

Ferries ply their way between Port of Spain in Trinidad and Scarborough in Tobago on a daily basis. Because of prevailing winds and currents, the trip from Tobago to Trinidad is much calmer than the reverse. The fast ferry no longer operates.

The ferry, *Panorama*, leaves Tobago at 11 PM, arriving in Port of Spain at 5 AM. On this overnight trip, you can stretch out in an airline-style reclining seat or get a cabin. Each area is comfortably air conditioned. First class even has cushioned armchairs and sofas and there's a bar on the first class deck. For snacks, there's a place on the second deck, but pickin's are pretty slim. If you can, bring some food along with you; that's what locals do.

The *Panorama* is large and accommodates cars as well as people. The ride is best on the first deck (first class) and will cost around $5 one way. Cabins are $14.

To take the ferry from Port of Spain to Tobago, buy your tickets between 7 AM and 3 PM at the Government Shipping Service Passenger Terminal opposite the twin towers in Port of Spain. Be there for boarding by 1 PM. The boat leaves at 2 PM and arrives in Scarborough at 8 PM. You can call for reservations at ☎ 625-3055/639-2417/626-4906. The trip from Port of Spain can be a problem for anyone inclined to sea sickness. I didn't find the trip troublesome, but almost everyone on board was uncomfortable. Some were truly distressed. Though I'm a devoted ferry fan, there is really not much reason to take this one, when the trip is just 20 minutes by air and costs only $20.

Driving

Check your **insurance policy** and credit card privileges before leaving home to determine the coverage you will have when renting a car. It may save you money, but it may also ensure that you have the coverage you need. If you should have an accident, get license and insurance information from the other driver, if one is involved. Contact the police and call your rental company immediately.

In T & T you are required to drive on the left side of the road, as in the UK and other Commonwealth countries. No doubt, you will find it highly disconcerting to see traffic coming from all the "wrong" directions. It takes a little getting used to, but you can always pull over and let people pass if you're going slowly. Oddly enough, people walk on the left side of the sidewalk, too. Getting down the crowded sidewalks in Port of Spain is confusing until you figure out what is happening. Although left-hand drive is the norm, middle-of-the-road drivers are not uncommon. Be especially cautious when approaching a blind curve and do not be afraid to hit the horn.

A current **drivers license** from the USA, Canada, France, Germany, or the Bahamas will entitle you to drive here legally for up to 90 days. International permits allow up to a year's worth of driving time.

Gasoline costs 40¢/liter and one wonderful thing is that service stations actually provide service at no extra charge. It's like stepping back in time in the US and what a pleasure! Gas stations in Trinidad are easier to find than in Tobago. Pay attention to the tank to avoid being left on empty with no gas station open or close by.

Picking up **hitchhikers** requires common sense, as it does anywhere. In smaller towns on either island, you can readily give a lift to women and schoolchildren. Young men can be more of a problem. Use your discretion.

Remember to use your seat belt – it's the law.

Road sign

Trinidad Specifics

The Airport

Piarco Airport, Port of Spain, Trinidad. This is a small airport with duty-free shopping on your way in or out of Trinidad. The Tourist Information Office here is very good and well worth a stop. Piarco is 20 or 30 minutes from downtown Port of Spain. A trip into the city by taxi will cost you $20 before 10 PM and $30 after (taxi fares rise 50% after 10 PM). If you're going to a suburb of Port of Spain, the fare will be slightly more. Negotiate and agree on a price before getting into the cab. The only alternative transportation is a bus, which leaves the airport at 4 PM.

Car Rentals

Most hotels and guest houses will arrange car rentals for you and, generally, they will discount the cost. If you prefer to arrange a rental independently, here are two of the better agencies.

Bachlus Taxi Service, 37 Tragarete Road, Port of Spain, ☎ 622-5588. One of the most recognized car rental firms in Trinidad. Rentals should be between $35 and $40 per day, inclusive. They offer the added service of dropping off a car to your hotel.

Thrifty Car Rental, at Piarco Airport, ☎ 674-0542. Rentals will be about $46 per day (inclusive), rising to $50/day during Carnival. Thrifty will sometimes accept discount coupons from the States.

Taxis

Route taxis are great. They are inexpensive and will take you to your exact destination. Flag down cars with an "H" license plate. They are **shared taxis**, inexpensive, and a great idea. Small vans, called **maxi-taxis**, also ply the roads, but they tend to stick to prescribed pick-up and drop-off points. You can also use a **private taxi**, which can be picked up from hotels or called ahead of time. They are quite expensive.

If you are heading out of Port of Spain, you can get route taxis at the bus station near the South Quay.

Planning Your Trip

Tobago Specifics

The Airport

Although recently expanded, **Crown Point Airport** is still very small. On leaving the terminal you'll probably be besieged by taxi drivers. There's no line and it can be chaotic. Pick one of them and actively ignore the others, who will drift away. Although these drivers are harmless, the crush can be annoying after a long flight.

Car Rentals

Having originally planned to rent a car, we ended up with a jeep. It turned out to be a much better vehicle for the roads in Tobago. Road improvements are continual, but there's a lot left to do. For under $40 a day, you can rent a car or a Suzuki soft-top jeep. If you rent for a week, make sure you negotiate a better rate; you can save a full day's rental. Remember to keep your rental contract in the car. It has the rental agency's phone number if you run into trouble or want to keep the car additional days.

Renting a car seemed easier to us than it has been in other countries. It was quick, with no questions or cumbersome paperwork. If you have a problem with your rental, bring it back and the company should hand you keys to another car with a smile. If you should get a flat tire, there are lots of small places on the road that will fix it for you in 15 minutes or so. When you're done with the vehicle, drop it off and you'll get a ride back to your hotel – also with a smile.

The twisted and narrow roads in Tobago are perfect for jeeps. It takes just 1½ hours to get from one end of the island to the other with no stops along the way. Although it's a small island, roads are extremely slow once you get away from the developed western end, so don't underestimate travel time.

Rental Agencies

Lucas Rentals, Crown Point, ☎/Fax 639-7704. They have cars and jeeps, with and without a/c, for about $40 a day. If you are renting for more than two weeks, they'll pick up the car after a week to clean and service it while giving you a loaner. Good service is their goal. They also have a new Volvo 940 that comes with a driver for

$35/hour; for $100 you can be driven in style and comfort all around the island.

Rollocks Car Rental Service, next to Crown Point Airport, ☎ 639-0328. Rollock's will deliver cars and has a great record for service. They man their phone lines 24 hours a day in case you have a problem. Just give them a call and they'll be there to take care of it.

Speedy Rentals Co., Ltd., Store Bay Local Road, Crown Point, ☎ 639-7038. These folks are a few blocks from the airport, so rental fees are sometimes lower.

Across the street from the Crown Point Airport on the left side is a small building with a car rental service. At the same place you can rent bikes for about $7 a day. Motorscooters and motorbikes are available too, but distances are great enough and roads bad enough that a car or jeep is a better idea.

Buses

A ride from Crown Point to Scarborough will take a half-hour and will cost 50¢. You have to purchase your bus pass prior to boarding. Sales points for the tickets change regularly, but as of this writing they could be bought inside the airport. Ask Tobagonians where to get them and you may find a location closer to your hotel. It's a good idea to buy a few extras while you're there because you can't ride without them. Buses leave every half-hour or so in each direction. Leaving from the airport area in Crown Point, you will arrive at the bus station in Scarborough, where you can make connections on buses plying their routes all over the island. The bus station in Scarborough is just behind the shopping mall.

Taxis

Taxi service on Tobago, whether private or shared, takes a while to figure out. Taxi stands exist at most of the larger hotels and, while it is convenient to hop in and go, it can get expensive if you use them frequently. Cars with license plates that begin with an "H" are taxis, private or shared. Plates beginning with a "P" are private cars. As an alternative to hotel taxis, consider using **route taxis**, which will pick you up if you flag them down by the side of the road. Rides often cost us $5 our first few days on the island, when we were using hotel taxis. The same trip cost just $1 by the time we figured out how to use the route taxis. Most of the taxis you'll see are shared route taxis, a very easy and affordable way to get around. For instance, a ride from the airport at Crown Point to Scarborough will cost only $1 per person.

Shared taxis are the most common way for islanders to get around. They are inexpensive and they'll drop you off where you want, even if it's a little out of the way. These taxis are not in bad shape and they don't overcrowd as they do in some countries. We found them a great alternative to driving ourselves.

Locals will also stop to give you a ride and you can settle on a price before setting off. We would never dream of getting into a stranger's car in the States, but it is quite safe to do so in Tobago. It reminds me of my first summer on Martha's Vineyard, off the coast of Massachusetts. There was no way to get around the island except through the "kindness of strangers." It was a great opportunity to meet folks you wouldn't otherwise get to know and it was very safe. Don't hesitate to get out by the side of the road and flag down passersby. It won't be free, but it will be inexpensive and you'll have a chance to chat along the way.

Music & Carnival

You can't mention Trinidad and Tobago without talking about the nation's music, a vital part of the culture. Both calypso, which is an older art form, and the 20th-century creation, steel band, have their origins in Trinidad.

About The Music

Calypso is an expression of outrage, of humor, of criticism and frustration. It leaves nothing untouched and it is very entertaining. The calypso singer is the town crier of politics, the gossip of the neighborhood, the commentator on everything that's happening and everyone that's making it happen. From the neighborhood to national and international politics, to the person in the first row of the audience, no one is safe from the sharp witty tongue of the calypso singer. *Soca* is a more recent extension of the calypso tradition.

Calypso is more about words than music and the cultural sources for calypso are many; no doubt slave communication was one antecedent. In fact, the African word *kaiso* is now sometimes substituted for calypso in Trinidad. Whatever its sources, calypso is a vehicle for expression, a means by which the people find their voice.

In the United States and elsewhere in the world, calypso enjoyed a heyday of popularity. Remembering the music of my parents' time, I recall a style that made one think of warm climates and easy living. In the 1950's, many of the most popular tunes in the States were adaptations of calypsos written in Trinidad. The Andrews Sisters popularized one song called *Rum and Coca Cola,* which was actually written by a Trinidadian calypso artist. He received no recognition for the song until he made his case in court and won.

As part of the Carnival tradition, calypso singers compete for the title of Monarch. The calypso song must be new, written by the performer, and its verses must fit within the structure that defines calypso. These songs are often very political and no topic is too hot to touch. Social commentary, humor, biting anger hidden in the stylish turn of a phrase – all are features of calypso.

Tents were originally used for calypso presentations. Today, performances are given in halls of all sizes, but they are often referred to as tents. One of the most popular of these is a music hall called **Spektakula,** on Henry Street in the center of Port of Spain.

While calypso is about words, **steel band** or **pan** is about music. **Pan** music developed in the Laventil and Picton areas of Port of Spain in the 1930's. A ban had been placed on public use of the bamboo instruments traditional to Carnival processions because the bamboo had been used more to pound heads than to pound out a rhythm. With a need to make music, all sorts of things were tried as alternatives. The steel drums finally evolved as the instrument of choice. With an active oil and gas industry, there was an abundance of surplus or discarded oil drums. Used whole or in smaller parts, the drums are tuned and notes can be played with skill. The steel band is everywhere, with five or a hundred members playing pop tunes and symphonies. The old oil drum has evolved and the pans are now shiny with chrome and professionally tuned.

Steel drum bands also have their days to shine in Carnival, and band members practice long nights for months before the competition. **Amoco Renegades** is one of the more popular large pan groups. The Renegades pan yard is on Charlotte Street in downtown Port of Spain. A visit prior to Carnival will give you a sense of the level of commitment they make to their music and the artfulness of the director, who keeps everyone going in the same direction. We were impressed. You can visit almost any evening around 9 PM or later.

History

Carnival predates Emancipation, when it was a celebration that had French origins with upper class participation. Back then, Carnival meant masked balls, house parties, and street parading. Emancipation brought participation from freed slaves, who added a flavor of rowdiness to the event with street dancing and stick fighting.

Stick fighting has a colorful origin and is thought to have evolved from the use of bamboo sticks to fight fires in the cane fields. It was a popular sporting event well before the slaves were freed, and it continued and expanded after Emancipation, with organized groups fighting each other while singers egged everyone on with outrageous lyrics and barbed comments. The singers accompanying the stick fighters are considered by some to be another of the many historical antecedents to modern calypso.

While the French had a tradition of partying before Lent, the British had a strong tradition of Christmas celebrations. These two cultural influences have merged to a degree in T & T. Christmas is celebrated, followed by New Year's celebrations, and pre-Carnival events begin right after that. Competitions among calypso performers and steel bands lead at an ever-increasing pace to the spontaneity and creativity that is the Carnival celebration.

When?

Officially, Carnival takes place during the week preceding Ash Wednesday, but there is so much more. Those days are the crescendo, but the train is coming on for about two months before as pan yards and mas camps prepare and practice. You can almost feel it in the air and certainly it's what everyone is talking about.

Carnival is more than an event; it is a state of mind. Thousands of Trinidadians and Tobagonians work together in preparation. Whether local or foreign, you're quite welcome to jump in.

Carnival

Trinidad

Accommodations

There are relatively few hotels outside of greater Port of Spain. But the island is small, and everything you'll want to see is within a two-hour drive of the city. You will find a few very nice small hotels in Blanchisseuse, an area where you could easily settle in for a few days. Otherwise, the choices we've listed here all have a special appeal, something that sets them apart from the rest.

Location

Port of Spain offers a large variety of accommodations, from large hotels to intimate guest houses. While the city may not appear to be a good central location on a map, you should remember that Trinidad is only the size of Rhode Island.

Contrary to most expectations, the majority of accommodations are not close to beaches. Maracas and Las Cuevas beaches are about 30 to 45 minutes from the city and most people go for the day rather than staying in the area. Trinidad has more variety than many Caribbean destinations and you may want to spend beach time in Tobago, where there are plenty of places to stay right next to the water.

Carnival is one of the better reasons to visit Trinidad and a central location in the city will save you transportation time. But Trinidad has more – steel band music competitions, Moslem and Hindu celebrations, wildlife sanctuaries, yachting facilities, miles of deserted beach coastlines, and a variety of city attractions.

Other Considerations

Tax & Service Charge

An important question to ask when making reservations is whether the price is inclusive of taxes and service charges. Tax of between 10 and 15% and a standard service charge of 10% will add significantly to your hotel and restaurant bills. We have noted where taxes are included in the listings below, but you're advised to ask in advance.

Special Times Of The Year

During Carnival, expect to pay up to three times the normal hotel rate. You will usually have to commit to a minimum stay at this time, too. Other times of the year, hotel rates are quite reasonable, especially in summer when you'll save 10 to 20%.

Credit Cards

Most hotels and restaurants accept credit cards, but make sure they take the one you carry.

Handicapped Access

We have listed a few hotels with wheelchair access, but there is great sensitivity to individual needs in T & T and there may be other hotels that would suit you just fine. If you have special needs, be sure to ask in advance if the hotel can accommodate you.

Cooking Facilities

Fewer hotels in Trinidad offer cooking facilities than in Tobago. When making reservations, ask what specifically is provided when a kitchenette is offered; it can vary from a hot plate to a full kitchen.

Bed & Breakfasts

We've listed hotels and guest houses, but you may also want to consider a bed and breakfast. Unfortunately, these private homes go in and out of business quickly. For current information, call Grace Steele at **Cecile's B & B Accommodations and Reservations**, ☎ 637-9329. Grace has a B & B herself and has listings of government approved establishments around the island. There are lots of others that are unlisted. The best way to find them is to pick an area where you want to be, stay a night in a local hotel and ask around. Prices for B & B's are usually lower than for guest houses and hotels.

Note: In T & T, a small hotel with fewer than 16 rooms is called a guest house. This may be confusing to Americans, who generally think of a guest house as a family home with rooms devoted to overnight guests. Sometimes a guest house is just what you imagine, sometimes it's a small hotel.

All prices are quoted in US dollars.

Downtown Port of Spain

THE ABERCROMBY INN, 101 Abercromby St., Port of Spain, ☎ 623-5259 or Fax 627-6658.

Owner James Thompson is very accommodating and always pleasant. What the hotel lacks in charm, it makes up for in its friendly and helpful staff. Deluxe rooms have a/c, TV, phone, refrigerator, and cost $35 single, $45 double, including complimentary continental breakfast. For the very budget-minded, James offers economy rooms with bath at $25 single, $30 double; for the truly broke traveler he has rooms with shared bath for $15 single, or $22 double. Prices do not include tax of 10% or service charge of 10%.

There is a small dining patio on the second floor where continental breakfast is served. The Abercromby is a good choice if you need to be in the city. It's also a good location for Carnival because it's just a few blocks from the Savannah, where many events are held. Car rentals are available to hotel guests at $45/day without a/c and $50 with a/c.

> **Amenities:** *TV, a/c, phone, free continental breakfast.*
> **Good for:** *Budget-minded singles or couples who want to be in central Port of Spain, especially during Carnival.*
> **Comment:** *The location is central, the staff are very nice.*

HOLIDAY INN, Wrightson Road, Port of Spain (mailing address: P.O. Box 1017, Port of Spain). ☎ 625-3366; in the US, ☎ (800)-HOLIDAY and Fax 625-4166.

This is a 235-room business hotel in the city center. It is exceptionally well secured and offers all of the services of a standard Holiday Inn. Standard rooms (single or double) are $99, and it's $9 for each additional adult. Children up to age 19 stay free of charge. These prices do not include 10% tax and 10% service charge. Suites are available.

One of this hotel's more interesting features is a revolving restaurant that sits atop the hotel. Built during the 1960's, the hotel has been well maintained, offers views of the harbor and is a good bet for the business traveler. One of the nicer amenities is their rain-or-shine protected tennis courts.

> **Amenities:** *TV, a/c, phone, pool, tennis courts, exercise room, restaurants, bar, free parking, business services.*
> **Good for:** *The business traveler.*
> **Comment:** *The location of this hotel may give it an edge over other business hotels.*

PAR-MAY-LA'S INN, 53 Picton St., Port of Spain, ☎ 628-2008 or Fax 628-4707.

This small guest house, like the Abercromby, is ideally suited for Carnival. Owners, Ramganie Bob Gopee and his wife Pamela, will do their best to make your stay pleasant. Rooms are a good size and simply furnished. The hotel is on the second floor and there's a large veranda for catching the evening breeze. Par-May-La's is set in a quiet residential area in the city with small restaurants nearby. Rates, including an American or local-style breakfast, are $35 single or $55 double. An extra person or child over 12 is an additional $10. Reasonably priced car rentals are available to guests.

> **Amenities:** *TV, a/c, phone, breakfast included, car rentals.*
> **Good for:** *Budget singles or couples.*
> **Comment:** *This is an inexpensive centrally located small hotel, where you will be made to feel at home.*

TRINIDAD HILTON, Lady Young Road, Belmont Hill, Port of Spain (mailing address: P.O. Box 442, Port of Spain). ☎ 624-3211, ext. 6042 for reservations; in the US, ☎ (800) Hiltons, Fax 624-4485.

Rooms are pleasantly furnished and some have great views from their small terraces. The hotel has all the usual amenities you would expect of a Hilton, along with a very large pool and lighted tennis courts. Rack rates or published rates for standard rooms are $141 single and $168 double or $163 and $187 for deluxe rooms. Room rates do not include 10% VAT, 10% service charge and a $1.95 per-day charge for energy.

This 400-room hotel sits high on a hill overlooking the Savannah with views all the way to the sea. Business services – fax, computer hookups, 24-hour Telex, worldwide courier service, secretarial and translation services – are available. Many business travelers find the Hilton convenient because it is only a short distance to the business district. Note: The Hilton's room rates do not dramatically increase during Carnival. At any other time of the year, do not hesitate to ask about discounts, which are readily available.

> **Amenities:** *TV, a/c, phone, mini-bar, restaurants, large pool, business services.*
>
> **Good for:** *Business travelers.*
>
> **Comment:** *If you like Hiltons, you'll like this one. It has a great location.*

Larger Port of Spain

CARNETTA'S HOUSE, 28 Scotland Terrace, Andalusia, Maraval, ☎ 628-2732 or Fax 628-7717.

Retired owners Winston and Carnetta Borrel have five guest rooms on their nicely landscaped grounds. Room prices are $40 single and $45 double. Kitchenettes are available. Prices do not include 15% tax and 10% service charge.

There is a small dining area for breakfast and light meals. Winston, former Director of Tourism, and his charming wife will gladly help to plan your visit. Both are great gardeners and you'll be a part of their home during your stay.

> **Amenities:** *TV, a/c, phone, kitchenettes.*
>
> **Good for:** *Singles or couples new to Trinidad.*
>
> **Comment:** *A good choice for the first time visitor looking for an easy introduction to a new country and culture.*

KAPOK HOTEL, 16-18 Cotton Hill, St. Clair, ☎ 622-6441 or Fax 622-9677. Toll-free from the US and Canada, ☎ 800-344-1212; from Britain, ☎ 0-800-951000.

Owned by the Chan family, the Kapok is run with every attention to detail. All 71 rooms in this nine-story hotel are quite spacious and have good views. The Tiki Village restaurant on the eighth floor has windows all around. It is well worth a stop late in the afternoon to watch the sunset and tale in the spectacular views. See the restaurant section, below, for more details.

A single is $76 and doubles are $89. An extra person or child over 12 will cost $13. Rooms with kitchenette are $79 and $92. Suites are $130 and $143. Prices do not include 10% VAT. The standard 10% service charge is not automatically added to your bill, so remember to recognize extra services with a tip.

Just a few minutes from downtown and near Queen's Park Savannah, the Kapok is an excellent choice for anyone visiting Trinidad, but it especially gets our vote for the business traveler. Rooms have voice mail, direct dial phones, and a dataport for Fax/modem access. Business services include Fax, secretarial, computer access, copying, and several meeting and conference rooms with state of the art presentation equipment. There is always a taxi at the front door. Make reservations two weeks in advance (six months ahead for Carnival).

> **Amenities:** *TV, a/c, phones, kitchenettes, good-sized pool, restaurants and bar, excellent business services, free parking, car rentals, and tours.*
>
> **Good for:** *Couples, friends, business travelers.*
>
> **Comment:** *We were very impressed. The staff is friendly and professional, the rooms large and pleasant. This is one of the very best in Trinidad.*

MONIQUE'S GUEST HOUSE, 114-116 Saddle Road, Maraval, ☎ 628-3334/628-2351 or Fax 622-3232.

This small delightful hotel has 20 units in two buildings. Single or double rooms are $45 and kitchenettes, single or double, are $55. Some of the rooms have beautiful teak floors and all are attractive. The first building houses standard rooms, the restaurant, and an office area. The second building, up higher on the hill, has the larger units with kitchenettes. The second floor units have balconies, while those on the first floor have terraces. We preferred the second floor.

The kitchenettes come with all you'll need for simple cooking – fridge, nice dishes and pans, but only one electric burner. Monique's is one of the best small hotels we found. Even in rush hour, it's just 15 minutes to downtown. It is immaculately kept and very tastefully decorated. Everything here is well cared for, including guests.

Monique herself is a very pleasant lady. Her right-hand woman, Winnie, is a live-wire from Dominica who has figured out everything you'll ever need to know about Trinidad. She's great. There is a small restaurant with reasonably priced local food and opportunities to socialize with other guests if you wish. One of their rooms has been designed to accommodate handicapped persons. Fax and computer are available. Ask for one of the front side rooms or second floor kitchenettes as they have the best views.

Amenities: *Phone, TV, a/c, restaurant, business services, handicapped access.*
Good for: *Singles and couples.*
Comment: *We confidently recommend Monique's.*

NORMANDIE HOTEL, 10 Nook Ave., St. Ann's, Port of Spain, ☎/Fax, 624-1181/1184.

A family owned hotel (Fred, Anna and Christopher Lee), the Normandie strikes us as a delightful holiday hotel. Their 53 rooms are attractive and nicely appointed. There's a very pretty pool and relaxing after a day of touring the island would be easy here. Standard rooms with double or twin beds are $60 single, $70 double, but don't have much of a view. Superior rooms with two double beds are $75 single and $85 double; these are the best choice. Loft rooms ($85 single and $95 double) are great for families.

Business services include Fax, copying, typing, and meeting rooms. For the business traveler who is short of time, there are more convenient places.

On the grounds you'll find small craft and specialty shops, a bakery and the nicely designed La Fantasie restaurant, serving international, local and Creole cuisines. Modified American Plan, which includes breakfast and dinner, is $25 per person. Tours and car rentals can be arranged. One special feature of the Normandie is its commitment to cultural entertainment. They have a large outdoor space under the trees where musical and theatrical performances are held.

Amenities: *TV, a/c, phones, pool, restaurant, shopping, tours and car rentals,*
Good for: *Singles, couples, or families.*
Comment: *The Normandie is not a resort, but it sure made me feel as though I was on vacation. It's a great place to stay and experience Carnival.*

PELICAN INN HOTEL, 2-4 Coblentz Ave., Cascade, ☎ 627-6271 or Fax 623-0978.

This very funky place is grouped with the popular Pelican Bar, a restaurant, a squash court, and gift shop. Rooms are very basic with private baths and cost about $35 single and $45 double, including all taxes and service charges. A few rooms have a/c. Units vary considerably, so have a look around before settling in. We thought that rooms 23, 24, and 26 were a little more attractive. Weekly rates can be negotiated.

There's an open-air restaurant serving local and English pub food cooked by Molly and the bar is just downstairs.

Amenities: *Some a/c.*
Good for: *Budget-minded young social singles, friends, or couples.*
Comment: *For the not-too-finicky young and lively crowd.*

ROYAL PALM SUITE HOTEL LTD., 7 Saddle Road, Maraval, ☎/Fax, 628-6042 or 628-5086.

All 68 rooms in this hotel are especially spacious and comfortably furnished, but the suites win hands-down. They are attractively arranged, large, and include a fully equipped kitchen – perfect for small families in town for Carnival or as a base from which to see the island. The Royal Palm is also surrounded by restaurants and shops and is only a short ride from downtown. Standard rooms are $65 single and $75 double. Large suites are $165. Prices do not include tax of 10% or service charge of 10%.

Amenities: *TV, a/c, phone, kitchenettes, small pool, restaurant and bar, car rentals, and tours.*
Good for: *Singles, couples and families.*
Comment: *Good location. Royal Palm has one of the better suites we found.*

Elsewhere On The Island

Arima

ASA WRIGHT NATURE CENTRE AND LODGE, Spring Hill Estate, MM7½, Blanchisseuse Road, Arima (mailing address: P.O. Box 4710, Arima) ☎ 667-4655 or Fax 667-0493; In the US and Canada contact Caligo Ventures, 405 Greenwich Ave., Greenwich, CT, ☎ (800) 426-7781 or Fax (914) 273-6370.

Asa Wright is best known as a nature preserve, but anyone with an interest in the natural rainforest environment will be comfortable here. Their 24 rooms from April 16 to December 15 are $107 single and $162 double; in the winter season, December 16 through April 15, prices are $139 and $210. These rates include all meals, service charges and taxes, as well as afternoon tea and a rum punch in the evening.

Situated in the forest at 1,200 feet, this former estate plantation of 191 acres is a non-profit preserve providing a home to hummingbirds, toucans, bellbirds, manakins, tanagers, and the rare oilbird. See the *Sights* section for more information.

Florenca Calderon is the pleasant, informative office manager. Groups are often booked from the United States, spending a week at Asa Wright and a final few days in Tobago. The busiest months are December through April, the dry season. During this period you need to make reservations one or two months in advance – maybe longer if you want one of the two rooms in the estate house. All rooms are priced the same, but those two are the best. Each guest receives one free tour each day and, after a few days, you will learn the trails well enough to go off on your own. Handicapped access is available, but be sure to talk to them in advance if you have special needs.

Meals are very good. See Asa Wright in the Restaurant section. Meals may appear to be vegetarian from the reserve's literature, but they are not. They even have pretty good wines. Asa Wright is a lovely setting for a visit, with a knowledgeable and helpful staff, perfect tropical forest setting, and sounds of the forest to soothe you to sleep.

> **Amenities:** *Rainforest setting, restaurant, guided tours.*
> **Good for:** *Singles, couples, families with an interest in the natural environment. This is absolute Heaven on earth for birdwatchers.*
> **Comment:** *We were very impressed. Asa Wright is well-known to the birders of this world, but we could have whiled away a week or so very happily.*

Blanchisseuse

BLANCHISSEUSE BEACH RESORT, 6½ mm Paria Main Road, Blanchisseuse, ☎ 628-3731 or Fax 628-3737.

This new guest house has 12 rooms with bath. A single is $40 and doubles are $60, plus 15% tax.

Located toward the end of Paria Main Road at the Marianne River, the German owners, the Zollnas, have made the best of this tropical setting. Fishing is good and ocean swimming is nearby. The guest house consists of two white buildings with six rooms each. There is a large veranda for relaxing and rooms come equipped with mosquito nets.

The Zollnas have opened the small Coco's Hut Restaurant and Bar across the street. See under *Restaurants* for more information.

> **Amenities:** *Restaurant.*
> **Good for:** *Singles, couples, small families.*
> **Comment:** *If you want rainforest rather than ocean, this is the place in Blanchisseuse.*

BOUGAN VILLA, L.P. #4, Paria Main Road, Blanchisseuse, ☎ 637-4619 or 637-6491.

Bertram Blackman and his sister Sandra have recently built this small guest house under the guiding influence of their gracious parents. They have five rooms, three up and two down, all with shared baths, for about $30 a day. Two apartments on the water are in the works. These will rent for $35 all-inclusive. Rooms are comfortable and attractive. There's a fully equipped common kitchen and a grassy lawn right on the water with steps leading down to the beach.

> **Amenities:** *Beachfront, kitchen facilities.*
>
> **Good for:** *Singles, couples.*
>
> **Comment:** *These are very nice people and they'll do their best to ensure that you enjoy your stay. The new apartments will hang right over the beach and should be a real treat.*

SECOND SPRING GUEST HOUSE, 67¾ Milepost, Blanchisseuse (mailing address: P.O. Box 3342, Maraval). ☎ 664-3909 or Fax 623-4328.

Owned by Frenchwoman Ginette Holder, this guest house offers four nicely designed apartments, all with ocean views, terraces, and kitchenettes. The one cottage rents for $50 single, $55 double, and $70 triple; studio units are $40 single and $45 double. Prices include breakfast and service charge.

This guest house is set high on a hill at the edge of the rainforest. There's no a/c, but with the sea breezes you probably won't need it. With tiles, wood and antiques, this is a lovely spot. Ginette is still thinking over the name of the place and it currently has no sign. Ask for Mrs. Holder's guest house when you get to town and someone will give you directions. The room price includes breakfast with fruit, home-made cheeses, muffins, and coffee. Other meals (not included in the room rate) are available in local restaurants. Ginette also has a store in Port of Spain, also called Second Spring. Look in the *Shopping* section for a listing.

> **Amenities:** *Great views, stylish setting, breakfast.*
>
> **Good for:** *Singles, romantic couples.*
>
> **Comment:** *Blanchisseuse offers both rainforest and ocean. Second Spring gives you both in style.*

SURF COUNTRY INN, Main Road, Blanchisseuse, ☎ 669-2475.

Owned by Mr. Andrew Hernandez, Sr., the Surf Inn is a charming and romantic guest house perched on the hill. It currently has only three rooms, but they are taking time, planning everything right and planning to build a few more.

Rooms have either balconies overlooking the bay or terraces by the garden. They are not large, but offer a small fridge, a hot water pot for tea or coffee, fresh flowers, a mosquito net, and ceiling fan. Rates are $50 single or double, inclusive of tax and service charge, and include a full breakfast.

There is also a place to eat here. See *Restaurants*, below.

Amenities: *Mini-fridge, hot water pot, restaurant.*
Good for: *Singles and couples, especially romantics.*
Comment: *We thoroughly enjoyed our stay. Blanchisseuse offers more in the way of romantic accommodations than other places. Flowers in the room, pretty views, and candles create just the right ambience.*

Chaguaramas

THE BIGHT, Western Main Rd, at Peake Marine, ☎ 634-4427 or Fax 634-4387.

Five of the 10 comfortable rooms face a furnished patio beside the water. This is a yacht harbor, so swimming is not advisable, but it does lend a pleasant view.

Rooms are quite nice. Rate is $40, except during Carnival when it rises to $65. If you're having work done on your boat, room prices are $35 and $55, respectively. There's a good restaurant on the second floor (see the *Restaurant* section).

Amenities: *Quiet, a/c, restaurant.*
Good for: *Singles or couples.*
Comment: *The Bight is out of the way, but if you're visiting offshore islands or hiking in the area it's a good choice. Be sure to ask for a room facing the water.*

Las Cuevas

LAS CUEVAS BEACH HOTEL, Northern Main Road, Las Cuevas, ☎ 664-5045.

Las Cuevas caters to the young beach crowd, with 18 very basic rooms. Junior Peloi is the manager and he seems to enjoy running a no-trouble, fun sort of place for the budget traveler.

Rooms have private bath and a water view. A single room is about $8, or $14 with meals ;doubles are $12 ($26 with meals), all inclusive. Breakfast and dinner are provided. Lunch is available, but not included in the room price. Food is local style with lots of fresh fish.

Amenities: *Restaurant.*

Good for: *Young beach crowd.*

Comment: *You're only a few minutes from the beach in this small town and this is the only hotel in the area. Junior can arrange fishing trips.*

Maracas Bay

TRINIDAD MARACAS BAY MOTEL, Maracas Bay, ☎ 628-0055.

This motel, owned by Robin Maharaj, was not yet opened when we stopped by. It will have a/c and good-sized modern rooms with clay tiled floors and sliding glass doors facing the beach. Ask for a second-story room. A restaurant/bar is in the works.

Amenities: *Beach view, a/c, restaurant/ bar.*

Good for: *Couples, friends.*

Comment: *Unavailable.*

Mayaro

AZEE'S HOTEL & RESTAURANT, Eastern Main Rd, Mayaro, ☎ 630-4619.

This very clean modern small hotel offers a/c and cable TV and is only a block from the beach down a sandy road. Rooms are about $43, single or double, all inclusive. There's a surprisingly formal restaurant/bar as well, with great a/c to beat the heat. Dinners are between $6 and $10 and lunch is $4-9. Breakfast is about $4.

Amenities: *TV, a/c, restaurant, beach access.*

Good for: *Couples, friends.*

Comment: *There's not much available on this coastline and Azee's came as a surprise. It's not a destination in and of itself, but if you're passing by and want to stay in the area, you should be comfortable here.*

Grand Riviere

MT. PLAISIR ESTATE HOTEL, Grand Riviere, one hour past Toco, ☎ 670-8381 or Fax 680-4553.

This Italian-owned guest house is easy to miss (we did). If you are looking for something in this northeast corner of Trinidad, it is one of the very few places available. Rooms are about $64.

Amenities: *Beach.*
Good for: *Anyone wanting accommodations in this area.*
Comment: *Not visited.*

Tunapuna

MOUNT ST. BENEDICT GUEST HOUSE (PAX GUEST HOUSE),
Mt. St. Benedict, Tunapuna, ☎/Fax: 662-4084.

Pax is an independently owned guest house, but it is set on the extensive grounds of a Benedictine monastery. The 18 rooms are monastically furnished, with large windows and great views. Only five have private baths. Single rooms are $56 and doubles $90, including breakfast and dinner. Set high in the hills, Pax is best known to birdwatchers, with over 120 species found on the grounds. The nearby trails might allow you to see trogans, manakins, and honeycreepers.

Built originally as housing for the monastery, Pax is now non-sectarian, but it still has the feel of a spiritual retreat. Tours to other sights in Trinidad can be arranged and car rentals are available. They do not accept credit cards.

Amenities: *Great views, restaurant, birdwatching trails,*
car rentals, tours.
Good for: *Birdwatchers.*
Comment: *This is not a place to kick up your heels!*

Camping

Camping may not appeal to many travelers in a lot of the back woods areas because of insects, heat, and creepy crawlies. We're avid campers though, and finally found a place on the beach in Blanchisseuse where you can pitch your tent or drape your mosquito net for under $2 per night. The beach has rough waters in the winter and is good for surfing. Later in spring and in summer things are calm and good for swimming.

The campsite we're referring to is on Paria Main Road. As you are driving through Upper Blanchisseuse heading toward the Marianne River you will find it on your left, just before reaching Coco's Hut Restaurant. Food supplies for an extended stay may be enjoyed as follows: Thursday the chicken man drives in, Saturdays the fresh vegetable man, and there's always great fresh fish. Tiny local shops can provide you with cokes, rum, and other sundries. The name of

Yachting

the place is Marianne Camping & Car Park. While there, we met Evette Olivierre, a very knowledgeable local guide who can take you up into the hills or to Paria Waterfall. Camping facilities are minimal.

Food

Fast food has overtaken Trinidad and most of the restaurants Trinidadians recommended to us served some variety of fast or already prepared food. Surprisingly, and for no apparent reason, Chinese food is far more expensive than other types of fast food in Trinidad. With a high percentage of the population being Indian, we were disappointed not to find Indian restaurants, where food is prepared to order. Most Indian restaurants serve *roti* and the majority of Trinidadians we asked recommended Monsoon as the best Indian restaurant – it's primarily buffet style or take out.

Natalie's Bake & Shark kiosk at Maracas Beach

All in all, our favorite foods were **local cuisine**. One traditional staple dish combines several stewed meats with a wide range of vegetables. Often served with rice, plantains, or sweet potatoes, the stews are rich with flavor, whether beef, chicken, pork, or fish.

We also love *roti* in all its forms. *Roti* is a large tortilla-shaped thin flat bread. It is filled with curries of all kinds and then wrapped up as a package. Unlike a filled tortilla, which is eaten rolled up, the *roti* package is opened and the bread used as an eating implement. You break off pieces and use them to pick up the filling. It's delicious. Sometimes you'll find the bread itself filled with dried chickpeas which, in our experience, keep falling out. It was good, but messy.

Seafood is plentiful on Trinidad, but one of the real treats of the island is shark and bake. This is a beach specialty with fried shark sandwiched between two fried dough halves. It's absolutely *delicious*.

Chinese food may also be considered local. It is different than the Chinese food served throughout the US, and you ought to give it a try. I can't put my finger on the exact differences, but the Trinidadian versions are tasty and widely available.

Note: MSG, locally sometimes called **Vetsin**, is used in many Chinese restaurants in Port of Spain. You can ask for your food to be prepared without it; sometimes they can accommodate your request.

If you're looking for familiar fast food, you'll find Pizza Hut and KFC franchises all over the island, but the local chains are better – **Mario's** and **Pizza Boys.**

Shandys are fruit flavored beers – sorrel, ginger, and lime. Like our wine coolers, shandys are low in alcohol and very popular. Made by the same company that produces Carib beer, shandys are exported to other Caribbean islands, particularly Jamaica.

Restaurants

Chaguaramas

THE ANCHORAGE RESTAURANT, Pt. Gourde Road, Chaguaramas, west of Port of Spain, ☎ 634-4334.

International menu specializing in seafood and steaks. Right on the water, the Anchorage has taken every advantage of sea breezes and is entirely open, with lots of rustic wood. Formal touches, such as white tablecloths, are not forgotten. They are open seven days a week serving lunch from 11 AM to 3 PM and dinner from 4 to 11 PM. Friday and Saturday brings music, dancing, and "liming" (T & T word for socializing). It's a busy nightspot for foreigners and Trinis alike. The menu is varied, with all dishes given colorful names: Dance the Moon is butterflied shrimp in a curry and coconut sauce; Buccoo Bacchanal is grilled fish lapped with a mushroom and wine sauce. They serve some interesting appetizers, along with the usual shrimp cocktail and a variety of salads and vegetarian meals. Dinner entrées range from $12 to $21 and an average meal will cost about $30 US per person with drinks. Tax of 15% and service of 10% will be added to your bill.

THE BIGHT HOTEL AND RESTAURANT, at Peake Yacht Services, Chaguaramas (west of Port of Spain), ☎ 634-4427/4423/4420. Only VISA is accepted.

Owned by Peter Peak of the Trinidadian air-conditioning family, this place is cool. They open for breakfast at 7:30 and serve till 10 AM; lunch is from 11 AM to 2:30 PM; dinner is from 6:30 to 9:30 PM during the week and until 10:30 on weekends.

It's a shame the kitchen ever closes. The drinks are strong and the food is as good as it is inexpensive. Breakfast is up to $4, lunch up to $5, and dinner can be anywhere from $5 to $22. They have a snack menu for between times that includes spicy wings at under $2 and fish and chips for $3. These were delicious, though the portions were snack-like, as advertised in the menu. The fried fish, covered with an herbed batter, is one of the most unusual I've had and one of the best. Don't miss the *accra*, fried dough with bits of salt fish served as an appetizer. It may not sound great, but it is. You can have a filling lunch with a couple of rum and cokes for under $10. The Bight is part of a marina and serves the yachty crowd and Port of Spain yuppies. There is inside dining, but the atmosphere is much nicer on the terrace overlooking the harbor.

BREAKFAST SHED, Waterfront, Wrightson Road, Port of Spain (near the cruise ship complex), ☎ 627-2337.

Local specialties are served at breakfast and lunch, with prices from $3 to $7 for a delicious meal. Similar to Miss Esmie's or Miss Jane's in Tobago, this is a staple for locals in the area.

LA FANTASIE, Normandie Hotel, 10 Nook Ave., St. Ann's, ☎ 624-1181.

The Normandie presents entertainment in its outside courtyard. Having dinner at La Fantasie first would be a great start to the evening. They serve nouvelle Creole food in a very stylish and attractive restaurant. Dinner for two will be under $50 and sometimes you can take advantage of their special three course dinners for under $12. Tax and service charge will be added to your bill.

INDIGO, Second Level, Rear West Mall, West Moorings (next to MOBS – see *Things to Do*).

Just opened and introducing tandoori cooking, the menu here is ambitious. The small restaurant is very stylishly decorated and the manager, Colin Davies, takes great pains to make sure it's a hit. He says current menu favorites are indigo chicken pâté appetizer at $4.50 and roasted chicken in herbed coconut entrée at $11.25. All main courses are served with fresh vegetables of the day. Lunch Monday through Friday is between 11:30 AM and 2 PM, and dinner, served every day except Sunday, is from 7 to 11 PM.

JOHNNY'S, West Mall, West Moorings.

In the mall food court you'll find several eateries. Johnny's is the best. Serving a fresh, inexpensive and tasty variety of local foods, Johnny's is popular with locals.

MARIO'S PIZZA, two shops in Port of Spain at either #1 Cipriani Blvd., ☎ 627-5464 or 57 Independence Sq., ☎ 623-5464.

This is a Trinidadian chain with locations all over the island. They serve pizza and other fast food to eat in, take out, or be delivered (50¢ charge for delivery). A family-sized pepperoni and green pepper pizza and two large cokes costs $10 to be delivered, and it's pretty good.

MONSOON, 72 Tragarete Road at the corner of Picton, Port of Spain, ☎ 628-7684. Indian food. Open for lunch and dinner from 11 AM to 10:30 PM; closed Sundays.

Their lavender neon sign outside is an indication of the stylish modern interior. Wednesday evening they offer a special buffet with several main dishes, vegetables, rice, coffee and dessert for $12 (tax included, but not service). Reservations can be made the same day. Their normal fair is a wide variety of curried meats and fish served with vegetables, rice, and potatoes as a *roti*, which they call *dhalpuri*, from $2 for chicken to $3.50 for conch. The same offering of one meat and three vegetables with "busted up bread" called *paratha* will cost $3 for chicken and $5.50 for conch. They have soft drinks, but also serve beer. Both the *dhalpuri* and *paratha* make a filling and tasty meal.

PATRAGE, 159 Tragarete Road, St. James (next to the Invaders steel band panyard). ☎ 622-6219.

Patrage has another, and most say even better, branch in El Socorro on Back Chain St., but it's pretty out of the way for the average tourist. The food at Patrage on Tragarete was just fine for us. Specializing in *roti*, it's another favorite Trinidadian restaurant. You can have your *roti* there or take it with you. Only $2 for a delicious filling meal.

PELICAN INN PUB, 2-4 Coblentz Ave., Port of Spain, ☎ 624-RHUM.
An English version of Rafters, serving English pub-style food with lots of beer. The Pelican is a great gathering place for locals and visitors. It's very informal, the drinks are cheap, and it's standing room only on Fridays. Usually this is the first stop on a Friday evening round of entertainment – next is a dance club.

PIZZA BOYS, Park Street, Port of Spain, ☎ 627-2697.
With locations all over Trinidad this local fast food chain serves burgers, chicken, Chinese food, pizza and ice cream. The decor is 1950's style, with juke boxes at the table and other paraphernalia on the walls. The pizza is quite good and everything seems fresh and inexpensive. Delivery hours are 10 AM to 11 PM.

RAFTERS, 6a Warner St., Newtowne, ☎ 628-9258.
Rafters is actually two restaurants set in two different buildings right next to each other, but with only one entrance. The first is a more formal restaurant with traditional white tablecloths and subdued lighting and decor. The second building was originally a dry goods store. They left the best of the old building and turned it into a very chic bar/restaurant with great neon signs for lighting, an attractive bar, and bar stools set around colorful tables. In all, they created a bit of home away from home for Americans, although this place is popular with Trinis as well.

The food is decidedly American and they do a close approximation. Service is excellent. In the restaurant they offer a roast beef buffet dinner for $21, inclusive of taxes and service. It includes soup, salad, entrée and vegetables, coffee and dessert. You'll recognize everything on their à la carte menu, with appetizers from $4 to $5, steaks at $18, and seafood from $11 to $22 (lobster thermidor). They are open for lunch and serve dinner until 10 PM. Uncomplicated good food is their mark. If you drive yourself there, take directions from the enterprising fellow outside the buildings. He's an independent and will watch your car if you give him $1.

TIKI VILLAGE RESTAURANT, at the Kapok Hotel, 16-18 Cotton Hill, St. Clair, ☎ 622-6441.
Chinese specialties at lunch and dinner and dim sum, a Chinese brunch, from 11 AM to 3 PM weekends and holidays. Reservations aren't required, but we suggest you book ahead if you want a window table.

This stylish restaurant is one floor down from the top of the hotel and has great views from its large windows, especially at lunch. Their pot stickers are very good and the entrées are all freshly prepared and tasty. They will accommodate MSG-free requests. Service is excellent. Dinner for two will be about $30. Free parking is available at the hotel lot next door.

VENI MANGE, 13 Lucknow St., St. James, ☎ 622-7533.

Local Trinidadian specialties at lunch only, except for dinner on Wednesday evening. Lunch is served on bright tartan tablecloths and will cost under $20 for two; dinner will be about $30 for two. Of their three lunchtime offerings, one is always vegetarian. Friday is the best day because this is a social gathering place to start the weekend. It's owned an managed by two very popular sisters, Alison and Reses Hezekiah. They are both considered bright lights in Port of Spain.

THE WISH AND TAKE, 78 Abercromby St., Port of Spain.

Open only for breakfast and lunch, this hole in the wall makes good take out local food. They have a few tables inside, but working people rush in and out during their lunch hour, box lunches tucked under their arms. A filling and fresh-tasting lunch with chicken will cost about $4 with a soft drink or a local fruit punch called sorrel.

Eating Out On The Island

Blanchisseuse

COCO'S HUT RESTAURANT AND BAR, Blanchisseuse. Associated with the Blanchisseuse Beach Resort, ☎ 628-3731.

This is a new small restaurant opposite and part of the Blanchisseuse Beach Resort guest house. The menu is local food with a German touch. Our pork chops were reminiscent of schnitzel. Be sure to specify how you want your meat cooked. Service is very slow, but the food is freshly prepared and if you're in Blanchisseuse, what's your hurry? Lunch or dinner with a drink will be $12 to $15 per person.

SURF'S COUNTRY INN RESTAURANT, North Coast Road, Blanchisseuse, ☎ 669-2475.

The Inn serves local food in a bar/restaurant on the hill overlooking the bay. It is a very romantic setting, like their guest house, and the food is quite good. Dinners are early, though, so don't delay. Lunch and dinner are both full meals; sandwiches are not on the menu. We had fish with sweet potato pie, black eyed peas, rice, vegetables and salad for two for about $32 inclusive. Everything was well prepared and very satisfying.

Maracas Bay

NATALIE'S BAKE AND SHARK, Maracas Bay Beach.

Fried dough is cut in half and filled with freshly fried filet of shark. This great meal will cost you about $1. This is some of the most memorable food we ate while in T & T.

TIMBERLINE, Maracas Bay Road, ☎ 638-2263.

Gourmet Caribbean food. At the Maracas Bay overlook just beside the phone booth, take the tiny road down the hill. This former cocoa and coffee estate is perched on a rocky outcrop of land jutting dramatically out from the coast. They are not open for lunch during the week, but you might want to give them a shot on weekends. We recommend lunch because you'll be there during the day for the great views of the coast in each direction. A walk along the birdwatching trails that lead down to the shore can occupy an afternoon and work off the lunch. The chef here will make you feel quite special, encouraging you to take a bite of the hibiscus that decorates your plate. Shrimp may be beautifully served in a banana leaf. These are just some of the touches that make the harrowing drive down to Timberline worth it, not to mention their home-made wine. The Timberline is also a guest house, but until renovations are completed, think of it as a delightful restaurant. Dinner is reasonable at about $15 per person.

View from Timberline Restaurant

Things To See & Do

Evenings

THE ANCHORAGE, West Main Road at Gourde Road, Chaguaramas, ☎ 634-4334 or 634-4386.

This large restaurant/bar sits right on the water in Point Gourde. Friday and Saturday nights the place is hopping with live bands and dancing goes on until the wee hours. See *Restaurants*, above, for more details.

> **Getting here:** *Take Beetham Highway heading west out of Port of Spain. Follow that all the way along the coast, always bearing left when there's a choice. As soon as you see a harbor full of sailboats, watch for The Anchorage on the left.*

MAS CAMP PUB, French St. at Ariapita Ave., Port of Spain, ☎ 623-3745.

Opened 10 years ago by three brothers, this is the place where it's Carnival all year long. The small club is open seven days a week, with live music – Latin on Tuesday, calypso on Wednesday, steel band on Thursday, calypso or a band on Friday, a DJ band on Saturday and ballroom dancing on Sunday. Popular with visitors and Trinidadians alike, the music begins around 9 PM and goes on and on. Drinks are not expensive and there's tasty bar food.

> **Getting here:** *Heading west on Tragarete. Just after Hong Kong City, take a left on French St. Travel a few blocks to Ariapita and you'll see the pub ahead on the right (across the street).*

MAU PAU, Ariapita Ave., next to Mas Camp Pub, ☎ 624-3331.

Open from 7 PM to 6 AM, Mau Pau is a private club with gambling. Complimentary memberships are available to tourists. There are three club branches – Casa Nova in Tunapuna, T.J.'s in San Fernando, and the Crystal Palace in Scarborough, Tobago. The clubs are not large and all have a 1920's speakeasy flavor. Games include Caribbean stud, Caribbean poker, American roulette, baccarat, and blackjack. The latter has the player-favored feature of being able to double down on any combination of cards. Limits range from a minimum bet of $1.75 right up to $175, but vary by game and table. Higher limits may be granted to high rollers. Safety deposit boxes are available, credit cards are accepted, there's food and drink, and taxi service can be arranged. They even have slot machines that may not be what you're used to, but are inexpensive to play.

Getting here: *See Mas Camp Pub, above.*

MOON OVER BOURBON STREET, (MOBS) – West Mall rear upper level, West Moorings, Port of Spain, ☎ 637-3448.

MOBS offers live music – from jazz to reggae to hiphop – in an informal outside setting on the second floor of the mall. A good selection of bar foods is available. MOBS gets a mix of tourists and sophisticated Trinidadians. Open from 7 PM to at least 2 AM. The mall is fenced and very secure, so leaving the bar at a late hour is quite safe.

Getting here: *Leave Port of Spain on Beetham Highway heading west. You'll be there in about 10 minutes.*

NORMANDIE HOTEL, 10 Nook Ave., St. Ann's, ☎ 624-1181.

Contact them to see what's scheduled during your time in Trinidad. They offer a variety of interesting musical and theatrical performances in an outdoor setting under the trees.

Getting here: *You'll have to ask someone (and maybe several people). We got lost big time.*

PIER ONE, West Main Road, Chaguaramas, ☎ 634-4472.

A private club open to foreigners. Pier One is on the water and a good spot for drinks and liming on the weekends.

Getting here: *Leave Port of Spain on Beetham Highway heading west. Bear to the left whenever there's a choice. Just past the Kayak Centre on your left you'll find Pier One.*

SPEKTAKULA FORUM, 111-117 Henry St., downtown Port of Spain, ☎ 623-2870/0125.

This is a large hall for calypso performances. It has seating for 3,000 and an inside bar. Set yourself down for some very amusing and stimulating entertainment. Calypso has its own form and structure musically, but most important is its lighthearted, acerbic, political and social commentary. No one is safe, not even members of the audience. Good fun will be poked at everything and everyone. It makes a great evening and costs about $5 per person. You can also take advantage of Ladies Night, when accompanied ladies will get in free. Lots of street food vendors are set up outside for intermission. Spektakula is only open for calypso shows from the first week of the new year through Carnival. There's no a/c, so wear something light. Parking can be a problem, but if you go early you might get a spot at the nearby bank parking lot.

Sights

Port of Spain Area

Botanical Gardens

On Circular Road (locally called Zoo St.), Port of Spain.

Across the street from Queen's Park Savannah, next to the zoo, the publicly owned Botanical Gardens date from the early 19th century. The 70-acre area is open during daylight hours. The gardens may be a little neglected, but with a knowledgeable guide to point out the interesting plants and trees they can take a few hours to admire. The gardens lie just outside the President's official residence and, if he likes greenery and flowers, we may all be in luck and the gardens may get the attention they deserve.

Inside the park-like setting you'll find a small graveyard where past colonial governors have been laid to rest. There is only one space left, awaiting the wife of former Governor Solomon Hochoy, a great friend to the people of Trinidad. Hochoy was a British political appointee who rose above politics on behalf of the people. During the week when a cruise ship is in port, it is possible to find a government guide (cruise ship travelers are often brought to see the gardens). For one of the best guides, see next page.

At the gardens you'll be able to enjoy the **Queen of the Flowers tree**, the national flower of Beijing, which has delicately scented red and yellow flowers; and **screw pines**, with inedible pineapple-sized fruit resembling the surface of the brain. The fruit's bristles were once used to make toothbrushes. The **Rocoo** was another cosmetically useful plant. It produces nuts containing red seeds originally crushed and used as skin decorations by the Amerindians. Later, the dye was used as lip color. The **Cassia Fistula** provides long string-bean-like fruit used during Carnival as an interesting form of music. **Samum trees** are the largest growing variety of tree in T & T and usually are home to a great many epiphytes. The bush-like **jatoo plant** has pretty purple trumpet-shaped flowers. Its seeds are boiled to make an intoxicating tea that is said to recreate a young man's libido in an older man's body. **Chaconia**, a beautiful red flowering bush chosen as the national flower of T & T, can be seen here too.

The **bloody beef tree** is an oddity. A scratch on the surface bark gives the appearance of red beef; the tree repairs these scratches quickly. The bloody beef is originally from Peru, where it has important religious significance. The **blood wood tree**, actually

Trinidad Sights

bleeds a blood-colored liquid that was once used as dye. The popular cinnamon tree is surrounded by a fence to protect it from greedy cooks, who use the spice heavily in local cuisine. Heliconia is a beautiful plant with heavy red, yellow, and green flowers, the colors of the Rastafarians. You'll see a lot of Rastafarian photographs showing this flower. The heliconia grows freely on the island in the rainforests. Date palms provide much needed shade. When the berries turn red they are harvested and used to make wine or palm oil.

There is a small area within the gardens that features plants with medicinal qualities. The leaves of the **Wonder of the World plant** are scraped to remove the outer skin, then heated and placed on swelling to reduce inflammation. The **chanallaner's** leaves are made into a tea that is used to treat headache and fever. The **wild sugar apple** is a fruit about the size of a large lemon. It has a speckled surface and looks warty, not round or smoothly shaped. While on the tree the fruit is poisonous, but once it falls, it is ground up into a white powder and either mixed with water and drunk or rubbed directly on a wound to relieve pain.

YOUR PERSONAL GUIDE

At the entrance to the Botanical Gardens, look for a fellow named Anthony Graves, a tall (about 6'4"), very thin, bearded, black fellow. He'll give you a great guided tour of the gardens, explaining what you're seeing and describing medicinal uses associated with some of the plants; once in a while, he'll even throw in local political gossip. He's very well informed and charges only about $10/per person for an hour or longer tour. We thoroughly enjoyed meeting Anthony and taking his tour.

Emperor Valley Zoo

Circular Road (locally called Zoo St.), Port of Spain, ☎ *625-2264.*

You'll find the zoo across the street on the north side of Queen's Park Savannah, next to the Royal Botanical Gardens. The zoo has good representation of local animals and birds, along with a reptile house and a relatively uninteresting aquarium. There are several species of small monkeys and a healthy variety of birds.

The facility is privately owned and appears very well managed. Animal enclosures are clean and most were nicely designed to accommodate the animal's needs. The terrain at the zoo is hilly and, since the land was formerly part of the Botanical Gardens, the plants and trees are quite interesting. We spoke casually with one of the park staff, Delbert Charleau. He was articulate in expressing his concern for public education and their commitment to improving conditions at the zoo. The curator, Mr. Kenneth Caesar, is doing a great job.

The Emperor Valley Zoo is a must stop for families and those interested in seeing some of the smaller wildlife of T & T and other Caribbean islands. Opened 44 years ago, its two sadder animals are the lions, given to T & T by Hailie Selassie some 20 years ago. The zoo is open from 9:30 AM to 5:30 PM and admission for adults is under $1.

Magnificent Seven
Circular Road, Port of Spain

Along the west side of Queen's Park Savanna, you'll see seven large architecturally exuberant colonial buildings. They are not open to the public and most need work. Some are being restored now and should be quite spectacular when finished. Among the seven are Queen's Royal College and Whitehall, the office of the Prime Minister. If you're in Port of Spain for a few days, you'll probably ride by them several times just going from place to place.

National Museum
117 Frederick St. at the corner of Keate, Port of Spain, ☎ *623-5941.*

Open 10 AM to 6 PM Tuesday through Sunday, the museum is free and offers exhibits on island geography, history, and art. It also displays a collection of Carnival costumes.

Old Police Station
Opposite the Red House on St. Vincent,
between Sackville and Queen Streets, Port of Spain.

This 1876 structure looks rather like a church or convent that is now a ruin. In fact, it was designed to be and always was the Port of Spain police station. During the coup attempt in 1990 the building was blown up, causing extensive damage. The new police station is across the street.

You may notice a Star of David on the building with a dove at its center. This is the police symbol in T & T. Apparently, the first police commissioner in Trinidad was Jewish. He convinced people that the Star of David he wore was a good luck symbol. It was accepted for the police insignia and is still used. Until recently the Star of David was also found on the four corners of postage stamps in T & T.

Queen's Park Savannah

Northern side of Port of Spain.

This city park of 199 acres has a race course and cricket fields. It was once a sugar plantation.

Queen's Royal College

See *Magnificent Seven* – Queen's Park Savannah, Port of Spain.

Red House

Abercromby St., between Knox and Hart Streets

This is the familiar name for the Parliament Building across from the old police station, in front of Woodford Square.

Whitehall

See *Magnificent Seven* – Queen's Park Savannah, Port of Spain. This building houses the Prime Minister's office.

Woodford Square

Abercromby St., Port of Spain

In front of the "red house" or Parliament, this public park, similar to the park in front of the White House in the US, is host to voluble speakers with strong opinions. Otherwise, it's just a park.

Elsewhere On The Island

Asa Wright Nature Centre & Lodge

Spring Hill Estate, Arima, ☎ 667-4655. Reservations recommended.

This 191-acre former cocoa and coffee estate was dedicated as a preserve in 1967. Very professionally managed, Asa Wright is a must for all visitors. A morning or afternoon tour is just $6 and includes tea or coffee served on the veranda, where you may observe at least 25 varieties of birds in gracious comfort. Hummingbirds, toucans, double-toothed kites, and hawk eagles are just some of the winged visitors. Sitting at 1,200 feet in the heart of the Northern Range, Asa Wright is home to many of the 400 bird species and over 600 butterfly species found in Trinidad.

Although you may have a chance to see some of the rare species here, the real heart of the place is its dedication to preserving nature in all forms. A network of trails that vary in length and ease of walking lace the grounds. An introductory tour takes 1½ hours and your very knowledgeable guide will cover the plants, insects, and wide variety of birds you'll encounter along the way. All trails, whether steep or gently sloped, are well designed to maximize your exposure to the wonders in this rainforest environment.

Some of the more exciting birds to see are the **bearded bell bird**, the **white bearded manakin**, the **golden headed manakin**, and the **collared trogon**. You may also sight a **tufted coquette**, a hummingbird, or a **tarantula** or **leaf cutting ants** hard at work. Behind the reception desk you will see two snakes in a terrarium: a **yellow rat snake** (or *tigre*) and a **vine snake,** locally known as the "horsewhip." If you have a special interest in snakes, speak with Alan Rodriguez, the Grounds Supervisor. If you're lucky, he may show you his collection.

Public tours are offered at 10:30 AM and 1 PM; the earlier one is probably more fruitful for birders. Two of the better tours are offered only to their hotel guests, one at 8:30 AM and an evening tour at 7 PM on Mondays. On the evening tour, especially during rainy season, you might have the rare opportunity to see a **peripatus**, considered to be the link between soft body worms (annelids) and insects (arthropods). The night tour offers a unique chance to explore the night sounds of the preserve and catch its nocturnal creatures in action.

A gift shop and library are housed in the main building. Asa Wright is also listed in the hotel section, above. **Special Needs**: A good insect repellent; cool t-shirt with long pants and comfortable walking shoes; flashlight; binoculars; camera with fast film.

Handicapped access is limited, but there is much to see and enjoy without leaving the estate house. Call in advance to make arrangements if you have special requirements.

Caroni Swamp National Park & Bird Sanctuary
Off Uriah Butler Highway.

A favorite with birdwatchers, Caroni is a huge brackish water mangrove swamp. The vegetation is unvarying and the boat trip through the channels to the swamp lake is dull. However, Caroni has its own special attraction – it is a roosting home for thousands of **scarlet ibis**, Trinidad's scarlet-red national bird. Until the mid-1960's the scarlet ibis, which resembles a small flamingo, was hunted both for its meat and feathers, which were highly prized for Carnival costumes. The ibis is now protected. You can arrange to visit Caroni either at dawn, when the birds fly out en masse, or in the late afternoon, when they return in small groups to roost for the night. You'll also see **herons** and **egrets**.

By the time you read this book, the Government Tourist Bureau should have completed a new visitor center. Tours of the swamp cost $10 per person. You can also be picked up and returned to your hotel for an additional $15 per person. **Nanan's** is the most commonly used tour guide (☎ 645-1305) for the swamp, but everyone charges and delivers about the same. Another tour operator you might try is **James Madoo** (☎ 662-7356). He charges the same as Nanan's. The trip is made in large boats carrying about 30 people; sit toward the front. Unfortunately, the noise of the outboard engine scares off much of the wildlife you might see along the way to the lake. Once there, operators cut the engines, tie up the boat and await the ibis. **Special needs**: binoculars; a telephoto lens for your camera.

> **Getting here**: *Leave Port of Spain on Beetham Highway heading east. Travel the Uriah Butler Highway south toward San Fernando and take the Caroni exit. It's about a 20-minute trip.*

Chaguaramas Development Authority

P.O. Box 3162, Carenage, Chaguaramas, ☎ 625-1503 or Fax 625-2465.

This office specializes in the natural environment of the Chaguaramas area, offering educational programs and tours. Bright and engaging, Dr. Jesma McFarland heads the programming and does a fine job. You'll be advised to contact this office for tour information or permissions at several of the sights listed in this section. If you're in the area, stop by and visit Fred, the seven-foot female boa constrictor. Fred has foiled attempts to release her into the wild by showing up in the backyards of neighbors looking for human company. She's lived at CDA since she was a baby. Back then, she was presumed to be male, hence her name. Her roommate is a caiman named Wally who seems equally pleased to be there. Boas are protected in Trinidad and Fred is part of the educational effort being made on behalf of these none too appealing creatures.

> **Getting here**: *Leave Port of Spain on Beetham Highway heading west. Stay to the left when there's a choice and you'll find yourself on Western Main Road. Follow along past the police station on your left until you see large greenish buildings on your right – the convention center. CDA is behind the convention center.*

Diego Martin Estate & Waterwheel
Diego Martin; no telephone.

The waterwheel itself has, unfortunately, been defaced by a fellow advertising his construction business in spray paint. There's not much else here, except some historical photos of plantation farming.

> **Getting here***: Head west out of Port of Spain on Beetham Highway. Just as you see West Mall on your left, bear to the right and follow that road till you come to a gas station, where you'll need to ask for explicit directions.*

Edith Falls Trail
Contact the Chaguaramas Development Authority at ☎ 625-1503.

Although in dry season the water flow is restricted, the 600-foot falls are spectacular. The trail is a gentle one mile, good for beginners or getting your feet wet as a hiker in the tropics.

Fort George
Just west of Port of Spain, off the highway.

Once a signalling site for ships at sea, the fort now has the remains of a jail and several cannon. The trip to the top is not long. If you especially like overlooks, this site will give you panoramic views. Otherwise, it's not particularly interesting.

Lopinot Historic Sight
Lopinot; no telephone.

A small town with an interesting historic sight – the estate of Lopinot. Lopinot came to Trinidad from Santo Domingo. He first owned land closer to Port of Spain, but in financial distress he set off for the interior and established a cocoa and coffee estate on this site. The small estate house has been restored and contains photographs and artifacts from the estate and some period furnishings. Cocoa is still processed here and you can see the restored drying shed. Martin Gomez is the estate guide and he'll give you a good rundown of its history. There are also caves in the area and local guides can show you the way. Lopinot is known for its people of Spanish origin and their music. They still make and play guitars and a wide variety of other stringed instruments here. **Special needs**: good walking shoes; flashlight.

Lopinot Estate House

Getting here: *From Port of Spain, head east on Beetham Highway. Lopinot is between Tunapuna and Arima. Stop and ask a local if you get lost (as we did).*

Mango Valley Hike

Arranged through Chaguaramas Development Authority, ☎ *625-1503.*

Maracas Waterfall

St. Joseph.

The falls are just an easy half-hour walk uphill.The rainy season increases the water flow, but even in dry season it's quite a sight. Water falls from 300 feet more or less straight off the mountaintop. No swimming is allowed at the base of the falls but, if you follow the water down, you'll find very chilly pools lower on the hill. The falls are religious or spiritual places for many people and you will see candles beside the path left as symbols of faith. Along the way you'll spot **parakeets, cornbirds** (black with a split yellow tail) **parrots, hummingbirds,** and **leaf cutting ants.**

Rock climbers might want to attempt the climb to the top of the falls, but should not do so without a guide. The rock face is very steep. At the top, you can cool off in an icy pool.

There have been reports of robberies on this trail and it might be advisable to have a guide along to handle problems of this sort. We didn't have a guide and no one bothered us, but you can probably stop in the small town and ask any local fellow if he'd like to go with you. Expect to pay about $5 to $10. Special needs: comfortable walking shoes; binoculars for the birds and butterflies.

> **Getting here**: *Leave Port of Spain on Beetham Highway heading east. Take Uriah Butler Highway north to Eastern Main Road and make a right. Turn left on Abercromby, bear right at the only fork and continue to follow Abercromby to Waterfall Road, the second right after the Catholic church.*

Mount St. Benedict Birdwatching
Tunapuna

Mount St. Benedict has a birdwatching trail leading uphill to a fire lookout. Just above the Mount St. Benedict guest house, by the monastery at the top of the hill, you'll find a gate. Passing through, head up the trail to the lookout far above. It will take about an hour.

> **Getting here**: *From Port of Spain, take the highway east and make a left at the Curepe exit. At East Main Road, make a right. Just before the Scotia Bank building take a left onto St. John's Road and follow it all the way up; whenever you have doubts about which way to go, stay on the larger road going up and that will get you there.*

Mud Volcanos
Devil's Woodyard

This is a sight I think I will never get to see. When first going to Trinidad, I read about these peculiarities and put them at the top of my list of things to see. Each return trip I vow to visit them and each time something gets in the way. They probably aren't all that spectacular, but I'm intrigued by the idea. We hope you get to see them and would very much appreciate hearing about your trip.

Nariva Swamp
Between Manzanilla and Mayaro.

Located along the mid-east coast of Trinidad, Nariva is a fresh-water, seemingly impenetrable mangrove swamp. There are no local signposts or visible entry points. Home to **howler** and **capuchin monkeys**, **water snakes** and **caiman**, the swamp is undeveloped for tourism. Nariva has suffered destruction of habitat by rice growers who cut areas of the swamp for agriculture. You can make arrangements to explore the area. See our *Tour Guide* section or contact **TIDCO**, ☎ 623-1932 for more information. Asa Wright, ☎ 667-4655, also makes birdwatching excursions in the swamp. **Special needs**: strong insect repellent; do not wear perfumes or anything scented as it attracts bees.

Northwestern Islands – Bocas Islands

Carera Island

Like Alcatraz, Carera is home to one of Trinidad's prisons.

Centipede Island

This is one of those small ice cream-scoop shaped islands on your left as you head out to the larger islands in this group. Centipede, as you can imagine, is known for its huge centipedes. It is also a roosting site for pelicans and the trees are covered with these large birds each evening. Hawks are also commonly sighted here.

Chacachacare

Still bearing its Amerindian name, Chacachacare was formerly a leprosarium and is now an island preserve. The island's historical significance is important, too. It was Simon Bolivar's jumping off point for the invasion of Venezuela. The leper hospital and its associated buildings have been looted, but you will still see much of the larger equipment and facilities that were left when it was closed in the 1970's.

The island has a good swimming beach, giant iguanas, a lighthouse, a salt pond, and manta rays offshore. For permission to visit the island, contact the **Chaguaramas Development Authority** (CDA) at ☎ 625-1503. For five people or fewer, the CDA charges $50 for the boat and guide.

Expect to spend about four hours on the tour. They can arrange to take groups out to the island or give you permission to visit on your own by arranging transportation through the Home Owners Association boat ferries in the same area.

Gasparee Island Caves

After a 10- to 15- minute boat ride, you'll be dropped off at a dock on Gasparee. Walk along a clearly marked cement walkway uphill for 10 minutes until you see the small visitor center. The boat will return for you at a pre-arranged time. Plan on spending two hours here if you like caves. Gaspar Grande Island, familiarly called

Gasparee, is the site of a very interesting network of underground caves.

The sight is open from 9 AM to 2 PM and the best time of day is between 10 AM and 1 PM. Elwyn Francis was our guide to the cave system and he is as knowledgeable as he is agreeable to be with. For under $2 per person, we walked across a wide lawn to the cave entrance, where stairs lead down. Lighting accentuates the cave formations. Over millennia, limestone was dissolved by slightly acidic rainfall seeping through the rocks from above.

At the entrance you'll see (and smell) some of the 500 or so nesting fruit bats that make their home in the cave. As you descend, the quality of the cave formations – stalactites and stalagmites – becomes more impressive, until you reach the base of the currently developed system. There, you'll see a crystal-clear pool of salt water, as still as it is pristine. If you watch carefully, you'll see leaves float very gently this way and that, indicating that the cave is connected to tidal action of the sea.

Pool in Gasparee Island Caves

The cave tour is limited to safe areas, but experienced spelunkers, may contact the **CDA** (☎ 625-1503) for a guide to accompany them into the undeveloped and more dangerous parts of the cave system.

Some of our friends and many other Trinidadians explored the caves as brave and foolish boys prior to 1972, before there were stairs or any safe way back to the surface. Diving into the underground pool between two large rocks was the game to play for the 8 to 15 crowd, and many have stories that tell of near-misses. You won't have those problems now, but the pleasure of seeing the caves will be undiminished.

Trinidad Sights

Getting here: *Leave Port of Spain on the Beetham Highway heading west; staying to the left when there's any choice. You'll find yourself on Western Main Road. Follow that for about 15 minutes, passing several boat yards, and you'll come to the Island Property Owners Association on your left (if you get to the National Guard base you've gone too far). Stop and ask for the island ferries. Prices are posted.*

Gasparee Caves	TT$90/$15.50
Gasparee-Fantasy Island	TT$55/$ 9.50
Monos	TT$55/$ 9.50
Balmoral	TT$60/$10.50
Domas	TT$65/$11.25
Parking at the Assoc.	TT$2

Arrival at Gasparee (Ramish)

YOUR PERSONAL GUIDE

A boatman named Ramish can be contacted directly to ferry you to any of the outlying islands. He's a good boatman and knowledgeable about the area. His home number is ☎ 634-4331. You can also leave a message and he'll get back to you to make arrangements.

Paria Waterfall

North Coast

The falls are accessible from Blanchisseuse either on foot or by boat. It takes about 1½ hours on a wide trail to reach the falls, where the brave can bathe in the chilly waters. In Blanchisseuse, ask for Evette Oliverrie at the Marianne Camping/Car Park on Paria Main Road. She knows the trail well and will guide you for about $10 a person for two (less for groups). The trip by boat takes 20 minutes each way. It will cost in the neighborhood of $52 for the boat, round trip.

Pitch Lake

La Brea

In the southwest corner of Trinidad, about 1½-hour drive from Port of Spain, there's a pitch lake. Touted as a "wonder of the world," its appearance can be disappointing. However, this small lake supplies road building tar to countries around the globe. It reportedly supplied the pitch for corking vessels during the time of colonial exploration. Widely believed to replenish itself, in reality it grows smaller each year.

At the site's parking area you'll be approached by many people offering to be your guide. Arriving in the afternoon will free you from the sometimes unpleasant competition for your business. To avoid problems with would be guides, go to the security booth and ask for assistance in selecting someone.

The lake is a puzzling oddity. In small areas, the pitch is liquid, while in other sections it resembles dry elephant skin. In small pools of water you'll find delicately fragrant lotus flowers. It would be a shame to miss this if you're in the area.

> **Getting here***: From Port of Spain take the Beetham Highway east to the Uriah Butler Highway heading south. Pass through San Fernando, staying on Southern Main Road, also called Trunk Road. Follow the signs to La Brea, the small town on the edge of the pitch lake. You'll know you're there by the deterioration in the road surface and by the smell. The trip will take about 1½ hours each way.*

YOUR PERSONAL GUIDE

To avoid all hassles with guides at the lake, call Marvin Billy, ☎ 648-7720, in the evening a day ahead and arrange for him to be your guide. When you arrive, simply ask for him by name at the security booth. He was our guide and we found him informative and easy going.

An hour-long tour will cost about $4 per person and tips are appreciated – unemployment is high in this area of Trinidad.

Marvin Billy, guide at Pitch Lake

Pointe-à-Pierre Wildfowl Trust

Trintoc Oil Refinery, Pointe-à-Pierre, ☎ 637-5145/662-4040.
Reservations necessary.

This private volunteer organization has the unique distinction of finding itself surrounded by oil refinery property. And the people involved are one of a kind, too. Committed to education, preservation, and an ambitious endangered species breeding program, their president, Molly Gaskin, and director, Karilyn D. Shephard, are impressive people. Deeply concerned with wildlife and habitat preservation, they are also aware that compromises and better solutions need to be found in a developing world. Believing that genuine education leads to positive action, they are committed to finding constructive solutions.

The preserve began with the idea of providing habitat for water birds, which an oil company executive had noticed were declining in numbers. In the 1920's, two man-made ponds were created and the 67-acre preserve was on its way. Later, the breeding program was introduced to ensure the survival of endangered species. Some of these birds, such as the scarlet ibis, formerly nested in Trinidad. Pointe-à-Pierre has six breeding pairs of the ibis, Trinidad's national bird, and has been very successful in releasing chicks into the wild.

Over 80 bird species are commonly found on the reserve, although it may take you awhile to record all of them. Some that you may see are the **wild Muscovy duck**, the **blue-winged teal**, **silver pintails** and **hooded mergansers**. Wading and songbirds also make their home here. At Pointe-à-Pierre, they are also breeding blue and gold macaws and they have several natural breeding habitat enclosures. There is also a habitat for the native caiman and another for a rainbow boa constrictor, a water snake found on the preserve.

Aside from birds that are native to the area, 35 of the 38 tropical bat species find a home here – insect, fruit, and vampire varieties. The initial tour takes a little over an hour and costs under $1 per adult. They like to have two or three days notice, but are flexible. There is a small building with film and video presentations on the second floor; the first houses a gift shop and displays of animals and historic artifacts. **Special needs**: binoculars; walking shoes; camera. Trails are not readily wheelchair accessible, although much can be seen from other areas, especially with a good pair of binoculars.

> **Getting here***: From Port of Spain take Beetham Highway east. Turn south on Uriah Butler Highway and go to the Pointe-à-Pierre exit. Turn right over the highway. The entrance is directly ahead. The trip will take about 45 minutes.*

The Saddle

A common name for the pass dividing Port of Spain on one side of the mountains and Maracas Bay on the other. The trip between the two is about 45 minutes.

Sugar Factory

Brechin Castle Caroni, Ltd., is locally called the BC Factory. Tours can be easily arranged by calling Joycelyn Palmer in the Public Relations Department at ☎ 636-2311, ext. 2700 or 2701.

This sugar processing plant is over 100 years old and operates only during the four- or five-month harvest season, January to mid-May. There are great opportunities for camera buffs, but be sure to bring fast film for the low interior light. BC is the largest landholder in T & T and sugar is a big part of their business. Cane is harvested either mechanically or manually and brought to the factory in trucks around the clock for processing during the season. On the tour your

Trinidad Sights

guide will take you through every step of the process, from raw cane to the final drying of table sugar. We found it fascinating and it would probably be a great tour for well behaved children over eight years old. Remember, this is a busy factory and there are no special safeguards for children. The BC Factory processes about 300 tons of cane a day and produces a brown table sugar, molasses, and a less sweet product used in the making of rum. BC is conscious of conservation and we were impressed by their recycling and reuse of all the byproducts. Our guide was Senior Level Lab Assistant, Kerryn Mohammed. He began working at BC as a laborer after college and has made a lot of progress in a few years. We also met Oscar Gooding, the sugar boiler, who took time out to explain the crystalization process. Everyone we met along the way was proud of what they did and pleased to have curious visitors. The tour took about two hours and we were excited all the way. It's a great opportunity to see where all that sweet stuff comes from.

Although heavily invested in sugar, BC is diversifying into citrus, rice, livestock, and aquaculture. If you're interested, ask if you can visit their aquaculture unit at the old Orange Grove sugar factory just off the Beetham Highway, between Port of Spain and the airport.

> **Getting here**: *From Port of Spain take Beetham Highway east to Uriah Butler Highway south toward San Fernando. After 15 or 20 minutes you'll see sugarcane fields. Watch for the Couva/Preysal exit. At the end of the exit, turn right over the highway and take your first left. After three miles take a left at the palm-lined entrance to the factory. If you're feeling lost, just follow the trucks full of fresh cut sugarcane.*

Turtle Egg Laying

The shoreline east of Blanchisseuse, which is no longer accessible by road, provides a nesting home to leatherback turtles in late spring and early summer.

Beaches

Beaches are not the main reason to go to Trinidad, but there are some good ones. One of the most popular is **Maracas Beach** in a town of the same name just 45 minutes from downtown Port of Spain. This is the closest beach to the city and that could explain its popularity, but it is also quite beautiful. Further up the north coast are other long stretches of beach, such as **Las Cuevas**, but the water can be rough here as you get into Blanchisseuse. The coast road ends in Blanchisseuse and limits access to more beautiful beaches like Paria, but you can hike in or have a boat drop you off for the day.

Along the east coast from Manzanilla through Mayaro there is a long stretch of beach, but the water can be tricky as it stays shallow for quite a distance and leads you further and further out. It is then that you can find yourself in trouble with the unpredictable currents.

Chaguaramas in the northwest was formerly occupied by a large US military installation dating from the Second World War. The military left in the 60's, about the same time the yachting industry developed, so water quality has to be questionable for swimming. Offshore, however, are several islands that have picture-perfect beaches.

Below is a partial list of beaches with road access in Trinidad. Hikers may look under *Things To Do – Sports* for less accessible beaches.

There are many opportunities to enjoy yourself on deserted palm-lined beaches, but be especially careful when swimming. Test for undercurrents and rip tides before you go out too far or become tired. The waters around Trinidad can be treacherous and they are often deceptively calm or shallow just before you find yourself in trouble.

North Coast

Blanchisseuse Bay

The waters are rough from December to March, but turn calm in the late spring and summer. Swimming near the mouth of the Marianne River is good and surfing in winter is popular here, but said to be better toward Toco. The calmer the waters, the bluer they get. Beaches here are relatively deserted, fringed by palms, and quite beautiful, set against a backdrop of lush forested hills.

Maracas Bay Beach

Maracas Beach is the favorite of Trinidadians. Recently, they did a great job cleaning and building all new facilities. The wide beach has white sand, lined with palm trees right up to waters edge. The new changing rooms, bathrooms and large restaurant make it very convenient, especially for families. Parking is across the street, where you will find small food kiosks selling bake and shark and other beach food. The bake and shark is tasty and will only set you back $1 or so.

Lifeguard stand at Las Cuevas Beach

Las Cuevas Bay

*Between Maracas &
Blanchisseuse*

In the town of Las Cuevas itself there is an attractive beach. The stretch is serviced by bathrooms, changing rooms, and a snack bar.

There is a lifeguard on duty in the main swimming area so you can feel a little more comfortable about the kids. Alternatively, you can walk down the long beach and be as isolated as you wish. Palm trees give relief from the hot sun. Watch for sand fleas.

Paria Beach

Inaccessible by car

After a 1½-hour hike from Blanchisseuse you'll find yourself on this perfectly isolated beach. It's an up-and-down hill walk, but well worth it. Ask for Evette Oliverrie in Blanchisseuse; she will be pleased to be your guide.

East Coast

Manzanilla Beach

In the small village of Manzanilla there is a public beach facility with changing rooms and restrooms. The beach is not one of the more picturesque in Trinidad, but it has a wild, windswept, deserted feel to it that you may find appealing. As you drive south, it runs on your left side for many miles. There is the beach, palms and little else.

Mayaro

It is hard to know where Manzanilla ends and Mayaro begins, except that you'll pass through a few small towns and find the beach becoming a little less wild looking. Other than its tamer appearance, it's the same as Manzanilla.

Northeast Coast

Toco

Toco and the surrounding area is densely rainforested and catches the Atlantic's winds and wildness. The coastline in the northeast is breathtaking, with rocky ledges and crashing waves. There are beaches, but most are better for surfers than sunners. If you are planning to spend time in the area, locals can probably identify a good swimming spot somewhere along this coast. It's a long drive from anywhere though, so if you are just looking for a swimming beach, there are better alternatives.

Sports

Deep Sea Fishing

In **Blanchisseuse** you can fish from the pirogues for between $52 and $90 per day. Ask at the fishing center across the street from the police station.

Fishing is equally good in the town of **Chaguaramas**, in the northwest part of Trinidad.

The **Bocas Islands** off the coast provide plenty of chances to catch the "Big One" and impress locals and friends with your tales of the one that got away!

Northwest Coast

Golf

ST. ANDREW'S GOLF CLUB, Moka, Maraval, ☎/Fax 629-2314.

Open at 6 AM, this 18-hole, par 72 course is hilly, with lots of trees. It appears to be well maintained. A nine-hole game runs about $18 and 18 holes cost $31. Caddies are available and you can rent clubs, but not carts. There is a pro shop on the grounds.

CHAGUARAMAS PUBLIC GOLF COURSE, Tucker Valley, Chaguaramas, ☎ 634-4349, ext. 129 or 145.

This is a nine-hole course that will take the average player about 1½ hours to complete. Golf club rentals and caddy services are available.

Great Speedboat Race

This is a mid-summer power boat race between Trinidad and Tobago. The course is over 85 miles and the direction of the race, toward Tobago, makes it extremely tricky, affected by winds and currents.

Health Clubs/Fitness Room

These facilities are now quite common in Port of Spain. Check at your hotel for the club closest to you.

Horse Racing

Racing is very popular in Trinidad. Contact the **Arima Race Club** at ☎ 646-2450 to check the schedule. They do not race year round.

Hiking

Trinidad offers trails in a wide variety of micro-climates, from dense mangrove swamps to mountainous rainforest to tropical forest, and just about everything in between. There are easy and difficult hikes and something to please everyone. Many of the easier hikes lead to spectacular waterfalls deep in the forest.

The downside is that there are hazards in some areas – both animal and human. Having a local guide with you should alleviate any such problems. Another alternative is to plan your hiking adventures with a group, such as one of those listed below.

Get in touch with the **Sacketeers Hiking Club** by calling Lawrence at ☎ 634-4284, Ricardo at ☎ 623-6292, or Garth at ☎ 675-1742. They have a variety of hikes from moderate to rigorous all over Trinidad, usually scheduled twice a month. The cost is about $1 per hike and you meet at a set destination at 7 AM. It's a reputable group and you won't be disappointed with the experience.

The **Chaguaramas Development Authority** in Chaguaramas, ☎ 625-1503, specializes in the natural environment of the Chaguaramas area and offers educational programs and tours. One of the hiking tours they run will take you to an offshore island, Chacachacare, where you can choose between trails to the lighthouse or to the salt water pond. Tucker Woods/North Post, the Covigne River, and Edith Falls are trails on the mainland. The Edith River Falls are a remarkable 600 feet high.

Note: Remember to bring plenty of water on any hike. Tropical environments can drain your reserves more quickly than you think.

River on the northeast coast

Kayaking

KAYAK CENTRE, Williams Bay, Chaguaramas, ☎ 633-7871 or Fax 628-1404. Weekday kayak rentals are under $4 per hour, rising to $4.50 on the weekends. Daily rentals are $15.50 weekdays and $21 weekends. Double kayaks are about 50% extra. Basic kayak instruction is $10.50/hour. Rescue, recovery, rolling and surfing instruction courses are available at about twice the cost of basic instruction. Owner/instructor Merryl See Tai has rates for groups and children, offering high skill-level kayaking trips as well.

Soccer

Very popular in Trinidad. Check local papers for games scheduled during your visit.

Squash

One squash court is available at the **Pelican Squash Club** at the Pelican Inn and Bar in Cascade. Call ☎ 637-4888 for court availability or see the bartender at the Pelican Bar right next door, who has the keys. The court is full size and has a good suspended floor. Usually, the court is open to members only, but you can ask permission to play; expect to pay $5/hour.

Surfing

Try **Toco Point** in the northeast or along the north coast in the winter months.

Tennis

Courts are available at the more luxurious hotels, but there are public courts at the **Princess Building Grounds** on Frederick St. in Port of Spain (☎ 623-1121). Public courts cost about $1 per hour. There are two all weather courts at the **Holiday Inn** and two lighted courts at the **Hilton**. Call to reserve court time.

Windsurfing

Chaguaramas Bay is the best area.

A Day's Drive

Renting a car and hitting the road is a great way to explore Trinidad. If you've never done it before, left-hand driving will require your attention in congested areas, but away from Port of Spain it won't bother you too much. The roads in some areas are pretty good; in other places you'll find pot holes that need a bit of care. Personally, we can think of no better way to explore and get to know this surprising country. As they say, good things come in small packages and it certainly holds true here.

One of the things that we found surprising was how clean the roadsides were. Every place we went, with very few exceptions, was clean. Another eye-opener is the wide variety of road kills you might encounter; it took us by surprise to see a six-foot crocodile (probably a caiman) just outside Port of Spain.

Traffic signs will amuse you more often than give you needed information. One of the funnier road signs is a big exclamation mark. With nothing else to go by, we finally figured out that it means there's a dip in the road ahead or a small hill coming up. A skull and crossbones sign indicates a dangerous curve. Much rarer are signs letting you know what road you're on. With relatively few roads to choose from, however, navigation is not much of a problem.

Below, we've given you basic descriptions of places you might choose to visit in your rental car. Most of these excursions can be very comfortably accomplished in a day.

Note: Avoid Eastern Main Road if you possibly can. It passes through heavily congested towns. The highway follows the same route, is in good condition, and is much easier going.

A typical country bridge

Trinidad Daytrips

Port of Spain To Arima, Blanchisseuse & Maracas

Leaving Port of Spain on Beetham Highway, head east toward Arima. You'll see an exit off the highway for Arima. We would give you directions through Arima to Blanchisseuse Road, but in Arima we got lost – hopelessly, as always. A maxi-taxi driver with all his passengers took the time to lead us out of town to the right road. We gave him TT$15 to have a beer on us when the day was done.

Note: You never know whether or not to pay someone for a service like this, but we've found that tips are appreciated when you say something like "have a beer on us," rather than just handing over money and saying thanks, which can be insulting.

The Blanchisseuse Road, where you'll find Asa Wright, runs between Arima and Blanchisseuse. It is a marvelous drive crossing the Northern Mountain Range, which separates busy commercially developed Arima and the tiny, quiet village of Blanchisseuse on the north coast.

The road itself is very narrow, a winding mountain trail that takes you through lush verdant rainforest. It is a feast for the eyes and for the spirit, dense green vegetation and almost complete isolation. We found ourselves in awe of nature.

Along the way you'll see nothing but the spectacular rainforest foliage, wild flowers, birds, and butterflies. If we could choose only one day's drive in Trinidad, this would be it. It has stiff competition from the drive to Toco, but the Blanchisseuse Road's surface is in better condition and the vegetation is spectacular. Also, this road is practically deserted; you might see five cars along the way, but no more. It's very easy driving, although you'll get lots of arm and wrist exercise on the steering wheel from all the twists and turns.

As you near the coast there is a quite fancy, newly built intersection. If you bear to the right, you'll find yourself in Upper Blanchisseuse, a very small village. Follow the road along the coast through the village and reach the Marianne River.

Over the river there's an old bridge with a sign that warns of its deteriorating condition. You can cross it in a car, but the road doesn't go very far before ending, and there are only a few homes on the other side. From Blanchisseuse there are hiking trails leading back up into the mountains and to Paria Waterfall. It's best to have a guide if you want to make this trip. Ask for Evette Oliverrie at the Marianne Camping/Car Park when you get to Blanchisseuse; she knows the hills well. Some rivers in this part of Trinidad have caiman, but the Marianne is said to be safe for swimming.

Turning around, follow the road through town once again and turn right at the fancy intersection. Following that road all the way will take you right back to Port of Spain, but there's lots to see along the way.

The road between Blanchisseuse and the next town leads through a bit of jungle with a few houses here and there. It's pretty quiet and along the way you'll see lots of heliconia growing wild beside the road. The plant looks much like a young banana tree with narrower leaves and the heavy hanging flowers are red with yellow edges. The heliconia is prolific in the rainforest.

Continuing along this road you'll come to Las Cuevas, another small coastal village. There's a public beach facility here, but the beach goes on forever if you want to find a more deserted section. Even right next to the public buildings there are few people on the beach during the week. There's one very basic hotel in town for the young and not too fussy.

Back on your way, a little further down the road and over a hill, you'll spot Maracas Bay. This is the most popular beach in Trinidad and it is quite beautiful. Fringed with palms, the beach has recently had an overhaul with new facilities and a general sprucing up. Stop here and have a bake and shark for lunch at one of the food stands to the left of the road. There's a small fishing village adjacent to the beach.

Fishermen at Maracas Bay

Trinidad Daytrips

The road from Maracas will begin climbing as you prepare to cross the Northern Range returning to Port of Spain. Follow the road up. You'll pass the Bay View Restaurant on your right (their name says it all), where you can stop for a bite or soft drink. Further ahead there's a wide spot overlook with a telephone booth. Right there is an almost invisible road down to the Timberline Restaurant, where you can have lunch on the weekends or dinner during the week. See *Restaurants.* Check your brakes before descending. It is extremely steep and once on your way you will not be able to back up or turn around.

Not much farther along you will near the top of the mountain and come upon the Saddle, a local name for the pass dividing Port of Spain on one side of the mountains and Maracas Bay on the other. Turn right to descend into Port of Spain, about a half-hour away.

Note: This is a very full day's drive if you do it all at once. Consider staying over in Blanchisseuse. It is one of the few really delightful places that also has lovely guest accommodations. See the listings under Blanchisseuse in both the *Restaurant* and *Accommodations* chapters.

Port of Spain To Manzanilla & Mayaro

Leave Port of Spain on the Beetham Highway heading east. Follow the highway to Valencia and turn southward on Eastern Main Road. You'll pass through Sangre Grande following Eastern Main Road and be on your way south.

You'll first find Upper Manzanilla, followed by Lower Manzanilla. Together, they form one small quaint village that looks a little run down. On our travels here, we picked up a few people on their way to the beach. They were carrying buckets to collect *chip chip* – the tiny shellfish native to this coast. As you first near the water, you'll see the official Manzanilla Public Beach. The facility is not as new as those found at other beaches, but it does have changing rooms. The east coast is relatively flat and it looks as if the waves to your left could wash over the road with just a little more wind.

Along this road there are many abandoned beach homes. It has the appearance of a town after a severe storm, but that's not the case. It is simply one of those areas that went out of fashion. A few houses are maintained, but most have fallen to ruin. There are coconut palm trees, the unending beach, but not much else.

To take a swim, just pull off to the left on any of the tracks and you'll be on your own private couple of miles of beach. The incredible number of coconut palms are used by the coconut factory

Old-style house

here. Along with the factory are some unattractive small houses built for workers and coconut husks litter the ground. There are more falling down and abandoned buildings.

Continuing on you'll arrive in Mayaro. This is a sprawling town with a few restaurants and hotels. The windswept beach dominates the whole coastline and Mayaro is no different. The only resort-style development on this entire coast is owned by the oil industry and operated for their workers, complete with pretty bungalows on the beach and tennis courts.

From Mayaro you can continue southward, with the coast on your left the whole way. You'll eventually get to Galeota Point, which we had hoped would be something really special. It might have been once, but isn't now. It has been completely taken over by the oil industry.

Following the road to it's end, you'll eventually come to an oil industry facility. There used to be a connecting route to Rio Claro, but the road has not been maintained and there are now impassable areas. From here, simply turn around and retrace your steps back to Port of Spain.

Port of Spain To Toco & The Northeast

Leaving Port of Spain on Beetham Highway, head east. Follow the highway all the way until it devolves into a two-lane road. You'll pass Waller Field on your right; take the next significant road left. The roads are not marked, but you can comfortably follow traffic because just about everyone will be turning left. Next, you come to a T, where you will turn right on Eastern Main Road toward Valencia. Valencia, which looks like a sizeable town on the map, is really very small. The turn-off toward Toco is right in the middle of town and easy to miss. Watch for the small sign. You will bear left as the main road goes south and pass through some small towns. Be warned: You'll see lots of road signs saying Matura, 1 km. After another 10 km (6.2 miles) you'll see another such sign. Although this can be a little confusing, there's only one road and it's hard to go wrong. Eventually you will reach Matura, which has a police station, houses, a health center, tire service, and a school.

Following the road out of Matura, you'll see a sign for Belandra Beach. Turn right for the short, but taxing drive to the gorgeous beach, which has significant surf. Fishermen here fish for shark, kingfish and snapper. Shark oil is advertised for sale on a variety of handmade signs along the road side. The oil is used as a liniment, massage oil, and "rejuvenator."

As you arrive in Toco you'll notice a sign for the lighthouse. It's not a splendid adventure, but it is worth a look. From inside looking out, the lighthouse windows are tiny and the steps get pretty narrow as you ascend. The lighthouse is an excellent viewing point to see the coastline in both directions.

Leaving Toco you'll pass through L'Anse Noir on a road with lots to catch your eye. It follows the edge of the ocean, which looks good for surfers, but not for

Northeast coast of Trinidad

swimming. You'll reach Sans Souci and continue from there toward Grand Riviere. Here, as the road leaves the coast and ascends, you will drive through an enormous jungle. With its towering trees, its hungry green arms could overgrow you in a careless moment. True jungle is remarkably beautiful.

Descending once again to the coast you will arrive in Grand Riviere, with rainforest at its back and seacoast at its feet. The small towns you'll pass along this route are not as memorable as the stunning natural environment.

Not too much further down the road in Bacolet is a sign that says "end of the road" and the road really does come to an end. You might consider staying in this area if you don't mind roughing it a bit. Ask around and you will certainly find a family with an extra room. In Grand Riviere there's a guest house that, by all reports, is fine. See *Accommodations*.

Now, retrace your route back to Port of Spain. On the road back you'll come to a small town with a brand new elaborate concrete bridge over a river with the ocean on your left. Cross the bridge and take the dirt road beside it to reach one more beautiful deserted beach. This one draws people on the weekends, and there's a woman selling roasted corn and a Rasta selling his wood carvings. Hot off the grill, the corn is delicious.

Note: The trip from Port of Spain to Toco will take about two hours, making it a comfortable round-trip drive in a day. You might consider bringing food along, as there are not a lot of places to stop for a bite.

Port of Spain To The Northwest Coast

On the Beetham Highway heading west out of Port of Spain, the ocean will be to your left. Stay on the highway all the way and, whenever there's a choice, bear left. Past the flour milling company, you'll see the Spectrum, a stadium used for big productions of steel band and calypso. Next, you'll come to the West Mall on your left. This is where you'll find Moon Over Bourbon Street (see *Things To Do, Evenings*, above).

The highway soon ends and you'll be on a two-lane, secondary road passing through a small residential area. Just up ahead is a place where you can rent kayaks (see *Things To Do, Sports*). After the huge cargo transfer and storage facility, there's a small beach, but swimming is not recommended because of pollution. Pier 1 (*Things To Do, Evenings*) is just around the corner. Down the road is the T & T Yacht Club, where you can stop for a quick, inexpensive and good lunch. Dozens of sailboats from around the world find safe haven here. A restaurant/bar/dancing place called The Anchorage is right around the corner to entertain you as well as the yachties. Every weekend there's music and dancing till the wee hours.

Just a little further on, you'll pass some large green buildings on your right and behind them is the Chaguaramas Development Authority. Further down the road are several yacht anchorage and repair facilities. One of these, the Bight, has a good restaurant and small hotel (see *Accommodations* and *Restaurants*). The Bight is a perfect stop for lunch or dinner, with very cool air conditioning and a lovely outside dining deck . Traveling a short distance further, just before the road ends, you'll find the Homeowner's Association, where you can rent a boat to take you to the outlying islands; one of the more interesting is Gasparee, with its caves. Take a look in the *Things To Do* section. *Note:* This is a pretty quick trip, just about a half-hour from Port of Spain. We found ourselves going this way more than once, to visit offshore islands and to have dinner by the bay.

Port of Spain To The West Coast

Leaving Port of Spain heading east on Beetham Highway, turn right onto Uriah Butler Highway going south. Uriah Butler is a divided highway in good condition. Just after getting on this road is the exit for Caroni Swamp, which you can see off to the right of the highway. You'll pass acres of rolling sugarcane fields and eventually see the Couva/Preysal exit (this is the one you would take to see the BC sugar factory). If you are in Trinidad in January or February, you'll be sharing the road with a multitude of trucks carrying harvested sugarcane to BC. Just before San Fernando, there's an exit for the Trintoc Oil Refinery and Pointe-à-Pierre Wildfowl Trust.

As you get closer to San Fernando, stay with the major road past the traffic circles (roundabouts) to Southern Main Road, also called Trunk Road. This will avoid the congested roads in San Fernando. Driving just a little further, signs will point the way to La Brea and the Pitch Lake. You can travel further south, but it does not get much more interesting. Return to Port of Spain by reversing your steps.

Note: The drive to La Brea will take just under two hours and is recommended only as an opportunity to stop and see the sights along the way – Caroni, the BC sugar factory, the Pointe-à-Pierre Wildfowl Trust, and the Pitch Lake. The drive itself is not memorable.

Shopping

Shopping isn't yet a high point in Trinidad, but there are duty-free offerings of standard fare – liquor and perfume – at the Piarco airport.

For the shop-till-you-drop crowd, Trinidad is going to be disappointing. If you are really committed you may find something interesting, but we have only a few recommendations to get you started.

Frederick Street in downtown Port of Spain is the central shopping area. You'll find lots of fabric stores with materials from east India, and handicrafts and souvenir shops. If you are looking for a mosquito net, pick one up at **Excellent Trading** for about $15.

Second Spring, 168 Frederick St., Port of Spain. Opposite the museum, Second Spring is open 10 AM to 5 PM Tuesday through Friday and 10 AM to 1 PM on Saturday. It's a small store offering great old treasures and some genuine antiques. Owner Ginette Holder is a French woman married to a Trinidadian architect. Ginette has opened a guest house in Blanchisseuse, also called Second Spring (see *Accommodations*).

True Value Mall, Circular Road, Port of Spain. Downstairs there's a food court with all sorts of local foods at reasonable prices.

West Mall, West Moorings. There are small shops with a few inexpensive souvenirs and t-shirts. There's a food court, where Johnny's looks like your best bet. On the second level at the rear of the mall is Moon Over Bourbon Street, a club, and Restaurant Indigo. The mall itself is a bit dreary.

Grand Bazaar Mall, Uriah Butler Highway. Brand new, stylish, and brightly colored, the stores here have outside entrances and extremely large windows. Open in the winter of '96, this looks like a good bet for the confirmed shopper.

Tour Guides

There are a few standard tours in Trinidad, such as Caroni, but there is so much else to see. Driving the island is the best way to get a sense of the diverse environments and the wealth of animal and bird life. Renting a car is almost a necessity in Trinidad; using it to explore far and wide is a great alternative to organized tours. If you are reluctant to drive yourself, hire a taxi driver like Krishna Arnie. We found him by simply flagging a taxi in Port of Spain and asking if he'd like to be our driver for the day. He agreed and for $50 he drove us for a solid eight hours. He was not only a good driver, but an interesting person and showed us features of his country that a more "professional guide" might ignore. Krishna would be happy to hear from you, though he is available only on weekends. His number is ☎ 671-2517.

Tourism is new to Trinidad. Though tour guide services exist, they may not yet be of the quality you would expect. For birdwatchers, especially, we would strongly suggest you contact Asa Wright, ☎ 667-4655. They lead tours not only on their own land, but also to Caroni, Blanchisseuse, and Nariva. We were extremely impressed by their articulate and informed staff.

Trinidad is blessed with a significant number of rivers for such a small island. Cliff Hamilton, Director of TIDCO, recommended river tours conducted by Steven Broaderidge, who can be reached at ☎ 625-1636. It's not inexpensive, though; a day-long river tour costs $100/person.

Birdwatching

Asa Wright Nature Center. See the detailed information in *Things to Do* in Trinidad.

Nanan's Bird Sanctuary Tours, 38 Bamboo Grove Sett. No. 1, Butler Highway, Valsyn, P.O., ☎ 645-1305.

Nanan's is most known for their morning and afternoon boat tours of Caroni Swamp. The boat holds 30 people and the twice-daily tours run early in the morning and in late afternoon. The tour costs $10 per person and they will provide transportation to and from your hotel for an additional $15 per person.

Coastal & River Tours

Kayak Centre, Williams Bay, Chaguaramas, ☎ 633-7871 or Fax 628-1404.

Owner Merryl See Tai leads kayak tours of the north coast through surf zones (in and out through the surf) with 2' to 6' faces. He also does combined kayak and land tours, such as Paria Waterfall where, from the landing site, you will hike up about 1½ hours to the falls.

In kayaks or walking you can also go with Merryl to explore the Nariva Swamp.

Steven Broaderidge, who can be reached at ☎ 625-1636, specializes in river tours.

Land Tours

Trinidad and Tobago Sightseeing Tours, Galleria Shopping Plaza, 12 Western Main Road, St. James, ☎ 628-1051.

An all-day tour of Trinidad will cost about $90; half-day tours are also available.

Tobago

Accommodations

Although not heavily developed for tourism, Tobago offers a wide variety of places to stay. The island is surprisingly diverse geographically and you'll find the character of various towns differing, too. Once you've decided where you'd like to stay, plan to spend time exploring the rest of the island. Tobago is a very relaxed place with warm and generous people. It would be a shame to stay at a resort and not see all the island has to offer. While other Caribbean islands have problems with crime and race relations, Tobago does not, and it's a joy to discover.

Considerations

Airport Transfers

Transportation from the airport is a service offered by many of the hotels listed, but not usually by guest houses. Hotels will either send someone to pick you up or will pay your taxi fare when you arrive. Check on this when making reservations. If you are not booking ahead of time, call the hotel or guest house from the airport and see if they'll pick you up.

Reservations

Reservations at larger hotels during peak times are recommended. At smaller establishments, you may not need to make formal reservations with advance payment, but you might want to call ahead and find out the likelihood that a room will be available. Right now, Tobago seems to have more rooms than it needs, even during peak times. While I can't imagine you won't be able to find a comfortable place on the spur of the moment, it may not be your first choice if you don't plan ahead.

Meal Plans

We have listed all hotel rates for European Plan (EP), which means no meals are included in the room price. Many hotels offer a variety of meal plans, but we have listed only the Modified American Plan (MAP), which includes breakfast and dinner, and Full American Plan (FAP), which features all meals. When making reservations, ask about whatever combination will suit your needs best.

Car Rentals

Most hotels will arrange car rentals for you whether they have someone on the premises or have to call a friend in the business. Usually, they'll give you a discount if you rent while staying at their hotel. See also *Car Rentals,* under *Transportation.*

What follows is a list of hotels, ranging from high-priced resorts to attractive and less-expensive guest houses. There are even a few budget accommodations that we thought were okay. All are clean, reasonably comfortable, and safe. For ourselves, we prefer small hotels with spacious rooms facing the ocean and we like having a kitchen. If there's a bit of charm or romance, we like that even better. Those looking for luxury and relaxation should find it at any of the great resort hotels listed below. We have also suggested establishments for those traveling with kids. These range from campsites to resorts. So, if you're stressed, or a family, or broke, or a golfer, or traveling alone, we've found the best choices to fulfill your needs. If you are handicapped, please see the notations for places that may accommodate your special needs.

Hotels are separated by the geographic areas described in *Trinidad & Tobago In A Nutshell* . In each area, they are listed in alphabetical order.

Crown Point

COCO REEF RESORT, Milford Road, Crown Point (mailing address: P.O. Box 434, Scarborough). Toll free in the US and Canada, ☎ (800) 221-1294 or Fax 639-8574 in Tobago.

Formerly the Crown Reef, this 135-room hotel was recently renovated and re-opened under the name Coco Reef. Although a variety of room styles, suites, and villas are available, we found the most appealing to be the deluxe rooms. Each has a small balcony and a view of the ocean. Coco Reef has been overly ambitious in attempting to create a five-star facility and more modest goals would have been attainable. Rack rates for deluxe rooms are $220 in winter and $180 in low season. Tax and service charges will add 21% to your bill.

> **Amenities:** *TV, quiet a/c, phone, a modest pool, beachfront, two restaurants and a bar, a spa, and two lighted tennis courts.*
> **Good for:** *Couples, handicapped access.*
> **Comment:** *More reasonable room prices in the future may increase its appeal.*

CONRADO BEACH RESORT, LTD., Milford Extension Road, Pigeon Point, ☎ 639-0145/6 or Fax 639-0755.

Store Bay Beach

Of the 18 rooms in this small hotel, the seafront superior rooms are the best, offering private balcony areas leading to a shared terrace for socializing. These cost $75 single or double, plus 10% tax and 10% service charge. Their basic seafront rooms have a smaller balcony and cost $65 single and $70 double. Meal plans are available with MAP at $30 per person. Ask about discounts for a stay of a week or more.

> **Amenities:** *TV, a/c, oceanfront, restaurant, terrace bar.*
> **Good for:** *Couples, friends.*
> **Comment:** *The Conrado's real appeal is its informal atmosphere and its proximity to Pigeon Point.*

CROWN POINT BEACH HOTEL, Store Bay Road, Crown Point (mailing address P.O. Box 223, Crown Point). ☎ 639-8781/3 or Fax 639-8731.

A single or double room at this 30-unit complex runs $76; a cabana is $89, including taxes. Managed by Jenny Aqui, this is an older two-story hotel right on the water. There is one long building with rooms and several duplex bungalows on very spacious grounds. What makes this hotel special is the setting. Stairs lead down from the grassy lawn right to Store Bay Beach. There's a small grocery store next door, as well as a fruit and vegetable vendor. After renting a car and exploring the island for a couple of days, settle in here for the rest of your visit. They have good entertainment by the pool a couple of evenings a week, usually Wednesday and Sunday. There is a dive shop, a ping pong table, and tennis courts. The courts have not been well maintained, but they'll do in a pinch and the hotel is planning to install lights for night games. All in all, I'd say this is one of the better spots on the island. You should book at least one month in advance and even earlier for Carnival, Easter, and Regatta.

> **Amenities:** *Phone, a/c, kitchenette, pool, open-air restaurant/bar, tennis courts, beachfront.*
> **Good for:** *Couples, families, handicapped access.*
> **Comments:** *Crown Point is an older style resort. It is comfortable, has necessary amenities, but is not glitzy. It typifies the relaxed atmosphere of Tobago.*

Crown Point Beach Hotel from Store Bay Beach

DESMOND & CYNTHIA'S GUEST HOUSE, Crown Point. (From the airport, turn right at Store Bay Local Road and the guest house is up a half-block to the left.)

This guest house is owned by two Tobagonians, Desmond and Cynthia Melville, who devote the first floor of their large home to guests. Their four units include one with three bedrooms, one with two, and two with one. All have kitchens and are quite pleasant. They charge $12 per person. Desmond has a great collection of island artifacts, both Amerindian and colonial. He has a wealth of stories to tell and will gladly take the time to share them. Many of Desmond's finds are in the museum at Fort George. They probably won't have a room unless you reserve in advance. It's worth dropping by to talk with Desmond even if you're not staying here.

Amenities: *Kitchens.*

Good for: *Couples traveling together, families.*

Comment: *If you don't mind being a walk from the water, this place is just fine. There's a nice garden and the place has a warm friendly feel to it.*

JAMES HOLIDAY RESORT, Store Bay Road, Crown Point, ☎/Fax: 639-8084.

Owned by a Tobagonian, this 24-unit hotel is conveniently located. A single or double room here is $40; the 14 apartments with kitchenettes and balconies cost $50 each. These rates do not include 15% tax. Rooms are attractively furnished, but seem a little small and there is no view. The James Holiday is close to the airport, beaches, restaurants, a grocery shop and fresh fruit and vegetable truck. Car rentals are available at the hotel and they have package deals.

Amenities: *Kitchenettes, a/c, pool, restaurant, bar, car rentals.*

Good for: *Couples, families.*

Comment: *This hotel doesn't really have much charm, but it's clean, functional, and centrally located.*

THE JOHNSTON APARTMENTS, Store Bay Road, Crown Point. For reservations contact Christopher Johnston in Trinidad at ☎ 627-1927 or Fax 623-8502.

On the grounds of the Crown Point Beach Hotel, these apartments are owned by the Johnston family. Sharing the same location and facilities as Crown Point, the apartments are less expensive and offer more space. There are two two-story buildings with a total of 32 units, all of which are very large with separate kitchen/living room, and bedroom. There is daily maid service and you have full use of all facilities at Crown Point Beach Hotel. All of this and great views of Store Bay will cost you just $50 per day, including tax, for a one-bedroom apartment.

Newly renovated and very attractively and comfortably furnished, their huge two-bedroom second floor apartment has about the best views possible of Store Bay and Pigeon Point. Including tax, the apartment is $200 per day. A similar apartment on the first floor with less spectacular views is $100. If you are in Tobago and are interested in renting an apartment, call Verna Wilson at ☎ 639-8915 to see if anything's available. Guests at the Johnston's come from all over the world and, of course, Trinidadians find it a home away from home. The hotel is usually fully booked in July and August, as well as during Easter, Christmas, and Carnival. Reserve well in advance for those time periods.

> **Amenities:** *Beachfront, full kitchen, use of facilities at Crown Point Beach Hotel (see listing above).*
>
> **Good for:** *Couples, especially those who like to cook, families.*
>
> **Comment:** *For a comfortable, but not fancy apartment on the water, this can't be beat. It's the bargain of the island.*

ROVANEL'S RESORT, Store Bay Local Road, Crown Point, ☎ 639-9666 or Fax 639-0328.

Just opened in 1996, this 30-room hotel is set on very spacious and well-landscaped grounds. The hotel is not on the water, but shuttles will take you to the beach several minutes away. Close to the airport, you may find noise to be a problem. Rooms by the pool are $125 and rooms with kitchenettes are $100, all-inclusive. They are pleasantly furnished with locally made teak furniture and very spacious. Owner, Sylvan Rollocks, started out on the island as a farmer and hasn't forgotten his green thumb. The grounds plantings are young, but very nicely laid out and within a short time they should be quite lush. One remarkable feature of this hotel is its elaborate water-saving system. All rainwater is collected in a huge cistern for use during the dry season. This forward thinking design is unusual and laudable. The swimming pool is one of the largest and best maintained on the island. Their restaurant serves local food along with steaks, and a meal costs about $20 per person, tax and service included. Car rentals and tours can be arranged and airport transfers are included.

> **Amenities:** *TV, quiet a/c, phone, full kitchens, huge pool, restaurant/bar, beach shuttle.*
>
> **Good for:** *Couples, families, friends, handicapped access.*
>
> **Comment:** *Owner Mr. Rollocks has thought a lot about the future with his cistern design and we suspect his new hotel will be as successful as his other ventures. The only downside is the proximity to the airport.*

SURFSIDE HOLIDAY HOMES, at the intersection of Milford and Milford Extension Roads, Crown Point, ☎ 639-0614 or Fax 628-4707.

It is not on the water, but this small two-story hotel offers large pleasant rooms with outside patios. If you're staying more than three nights, they'll happily take you to and from the airport. There's a pay phone on the premises and they sell phone cards as well. With Las Vegas lighting and lots of plants, the Surfside has a unique look. Singles are $30 to $35 and doubles $35 to $40. Weekly rates are negotiable.

The hotel is within walking distance from Store Bay and Pigeon Point and there's a grocery store and fruit and vegetable stand nearby. Meals are available for guests on request.

The manager is a nice fellow named Mohammed and his wife, Madhoorie (nicknamed Mads) is a gentle, lovely person and a great cook. She's often generous with tastes from her kitchen so it's good to make friends. The Surfside is great for anyone traveling alone or for social folks. There's a very friendly, open atmosphere, allowing you to make friends fast. Evening often brings gatherings where the day's adventures are shared, along with a beer or two.

You won't need a car unless you plan to explore the island and, even then, you may find another guest who'll take you along in their rental. The Surfside has lots of repeat visitors.

> **Amenities:** *TV, a/c, full kitchens.*
>
> **Good for:** *Sociable singles, couples, and friends.*
>
> **Comment:** *The Surfside is a good choice because of Mohammed and Mads, the owners. They're terrific and they make the whole place feel just right.*

TROPIKIST BEACH HOTEL, LTD., P.O. Box 77, Crown Point, ☎ 639-8512/3 or Fax 645-0341.

All rooms are spacious and have large private balconies or terraces with wonderful views of the ocean and Pigeon Point across a graceful lawn area. If you stop by without reservations, you have a decent chance of getting a room.

Managed by Mr. Balchan Ramsaran, the Tropikist is an architectural delight. Just down from the wide lawn there is a sandy beach from which to admire the sunset. (There is too much coral to make it swimmable; good swimming beaches are a few minutes away.)

A single or double standard room is $100 in the high season and $70 in low, not including 10% tax and 10% service charge. A spacious superior room on the third floor with external quiet air conditioning is $125 plus tax and service charge in high season and $95 plus extras in low season. MAP is $30 per person. If you are staying three days or more, special discounts are offered and group rates are available, too.

The hotel is just five minutes from the airport on Store Bay Beach.

Amenities: *Phone, a/c, pool, restaurant/bar, oceanfront, handicapped access.*
Good for: *Couples, families, friends.*
Comment: *The Tropikist is great. The staff are friendly, but not intrusive. Too bad the icy pool isn't heated. See also Restaurants.*

Mid-Caribbean Coast

ARNOS VALE HOTEL RESORT, Arnos Vale Road, Arnos Vale (mailing address: P.O. Box 208, Scarborough). ☎ 639-2881/82 or Fax 639-4629/3251.

This lovely 33-room hotel is popular with Italians. Rooms in high season are $110 single and $160 double, not including tax and service charges. Breakfast is $12, lunch $25, and dinner $35 per person. Ask about their discount for honeymooners (bring proof).

Meals are a real attraction at Arnos Vale. All dinners are wonderful European extravaganzas, starting with soup and moving to antipasto, pasta, meat, fish, dessert, cheese and coffee – seven courses each day. There is one seating at 8 PM for dinner and one for lunch at 1 PM. Breakfast is served from 8 to 10 AM and tea is at 5 PM. Service is wonderful, with everything taken care of.

This is a very pretty and somewhat isolated place, with extensive gardens and a quiet and protected environment, surrounded by hills. Arnos Vale is also known all over the island as a great place for snorkeling. The beach is surrounded by rocky cliffs that create a small horseshoe-shaped bay. It has an exclusive and very private feel. While there, we met Larry and Jill Shindelman from Washington, D.C., who had been to Arnos Vale three times, the first in 1968, the second in 1973, and this year (1996) for their third visit. They were very curious to see what had changed and were pleasantly surprised. Everything except the pool was the same. "The pool has become a bit Floridian, but otherwise it's paradise."

Amenities: *TV, a/c, phones, pool, restaurants, bar, beachfront, gardens, kayaks, tennis, snorkeling, volleyball.*
Good for: *Romantic couples (honeymooners), families.*
Comment: *If you are looking for a sheltered beautiful environment where everything is taken care of, this is it. It is small and the gardens are gorgeous. It is occupied by vacationing Italians who apparently only stop socializing when they are asleep. A quiet afternoon by the pool might be hard to find.*

BLUE HORIZON, Jacamar Dr., Mt. Irvine, ☎/Fax 639-0432/33.

Set above the Mt. Irvine Golf Course and overlooking Buccoo Reef in the distance, all rooms have well-appointed kitchens and patio areas. The hotel was nicely designed and built with ventilation to make the best use of sea breezes; a/c isn't necessary on a continual basis. The setting is high on a hill overlooking Mt. Irvine Bay and you can see all the way to Pigeon Point. This is a very pleasant small hotel with lots of opportunities to interact with other guests. It is a little out of the way though, so plan to have a car. Their 12 units include seven rooms at $50 single or $75 double. A deluxe apartment is $60 single or $90 double and their very spacious two-bedroom apartment with a large loft goes for $150. Off-season rates drop by about 20%. Prices do not include 10% tax and 10% service.

Blue Horizon also offers a barbecue terrace, grocery shop, and free ground transfers. Kameal Ali, one of the managers, is a very nice fellow and always ready to help. They've been open for three years and have kept everything looking brand new, except the gardens which are wonderfully healthy and well settled in. There is no restaurant on the grounds as yet, but the small Rolita Restaurant nearby serves pizza, and other simple meals.

> **Amenities:** *Phones, a/c, pool, full kitchens, laundry service, view of Buccoo in the distance.*
>
> **Good for:** *Families, couples, friends. For folks traveling with children and wanting a mid-priced hotel, this is a good choice.*
>
> **Comment:** *The views from this small, pretty hotel are great.*

THE GINGERBREAD VILLA, Plymouth (mailing address: Box 391, Scarborough). ☎ 639-4461.

With just one self-contained studio room, this is a small guest house indeed. More rooms are in the works because it's proved so popular. Sitting right by the beach in Plymouth this small house was designed and built to resemble the old-style gingerbread houses on the island, as the name implies. The studio offers a private bath, kitchen area, and patio overlooking the lawn and beach. A couple of mountain bikes are there for your use. Owner Eve Mendez has created a very special place at $40 per night.

> **Amenities:** *Kitchen, beachfront, mountain bikes.*
>
> **Good for:** *Couples, independent singles wanting peace and privacy.*
>
> **Comment:** *This is delightful private little place right on the water. Call for reservations.*

GRAFTON BEACH RESORT, Black Rock (mailing address: P.O. Box 25, Scarborough). ☎ 639-0191, or toll-free from the US, ☎ (800) 223-6510 or Fax 639-0030.

Situated on a steep hill, the Grafton is a full-scale resort overlooking Stone Haven Bay. As island hotels go, it is large, with 112 rooms, and typical of more developed Caribbean islands. Superior rooms have a view and cost $225/day. Off-season rates drop to $162. Meal plans are available with MAP at $41 and FAP at $51. About half of the guests arrange for FAP. Prices do not include tax (10-15%) and service charges of 10%. Rental cars are available and there is a taxi stand. One of their several restaurants, the Buccaneer, is right on the beach below the hotel. Rooms are nicely furnished, but they are not large. All rooms have balconies. You should reserve at least two weeks in advance.

> **Amenities:** *Phone, a/c, TV, mini-bars, pool (swim-up bar), several restaurants and bars, squash courts with a/c, gymnasium, hair salon, dive shop, beachfront.*
> **Good for:** *Couples and families looking for a holiday vacation experience with all services provided.*
> **Comment:** *This is a resort for people who like people. You can leave home and still have all the comforts.*

LE GRAND COURLAND, Black Rock (mailing address: P.O. Box 25, Scarborough). ☎ 639-0191 or Fax 639-0030, toll-free in the US ☎ (800) 223-6510, or in Canada ☎ (800) 424-5500.

On a steep hill overlooking Stone Haven Bay, the 78-room Grand Courland is right next door to and owned by the same corporation that owns the Grafton. It is a more luxurious resort than its neighbor, with all the amenities you could want. Their 60 deluxe rooms are spacious and have balconies overlooking the beach below. Furnished with locally produced teak, they have quiet remote controlled a/c and large bathrooms equipped with everything, even a scale. Deluxe rooms are $338. Rooms with an enclosed patio jacuzzi are $375 and one-bedroom suites are $514. Children 5 to 12 are an extra $30. Meal plans are available with MAP at $57 and FAP at $70 per person. All prices are inclusive of taxes and service charges.

There is a long pool for laps, but it also has a swim-up bar. The spa with sauna, hot tub, and massage will soothe you after a visit to their exercise room, which has a good selection of weight training and aerobic machines. You may use the squash courts next door and a golf course down the road.

Two distinct restaurants are on the premises. The open-air Pinnacle serves local and international dishes and the informal

Leandros features Mediterranean cuisine. Business is attended to with computer, Fax, and secretarial services. Conference facilities are available. The Courland has non-smoking rooms and services for the handicapped, which include on-site wheelchairs.

> **Amenities:** *TV, quiet a/c, phone, in-room safe, mini-bar, pool, two restaurants, swim-up bar, lighted tennis courts, fully-equipped gym and spa, beach access, business services, handicapped access, non-smoking rooms.*
>
> **Good for:** *Couples, friends, business people.*
>
> **Comment:** *This is a small resort. Rooms are spacious, well appointed and comfortable. All services come with a smile.*

MT. IRVINE BAY HOTEL & GOLF CLUB, Mt. Irvine (mailing address: P.O. Box 222, Scarborough). ☎ 639-8871/2/3 or toll-free from the US at ☎ 800-44-UTELL, Fax 639-8800.

Built on the site of an old sugar mill, this is an impressive 105-room hotel with 16 acres of well-maintained grounds. The hotel is large by island standards, offering rooms, suites, and cottages. Its most unusual feature is the 18-hole golf course that covers 127 acres. Taxis and car rentals are available. Their premier restaurant is the Beau Rivage, which is set in a separate stone building with a good view of the bay. When it first opened, the food at Beau Rivage was not up to its high prices, but they've since lowered the prices and improved the quality. We spoke with other guests who were very pleased with the quality of their other restaurant – the Sugar Mill. Standard rooms are $235 in winter and $165 in summer; cottage rooms $390 or $320 in summer; and one-bedroom suites are $720 or $510 in summer. Children under age four stay free, those age five to 12 pay $25 per day. Meal plans are available; MAP is $41 and FAP is $60. Although it is not right on the beach, this is a grand hotel and appears to be more luxurious than similar resorts on the island. Beach facilities for the hotel are just a five-minute ride away on Mt. Irvine Beach, which also offers a watersports shop.

> **Amenities:** *TV, a/c, phone, nice pool, golf course, restaurants, bar, beach, bar/restaurant, tennis courts.*
>
> **Good for:** *Golfing couples, people who like quiet luxury.*
>
> **Comment:** *This is a hotel where service and luxury are what it's all about. Golfers will be thrilled. It would also be great for small business conferences.*

SEAHORSE INN, Old Grafton Road, Black Rock, ☎ 639-0686.

Just across the road from the beach is the new Seahorse Inn, offering just three guest rooms and a large restaurant. All rooms are $80, which includes whatever breakfast you can dream up. Tax and service are included. The two front rooms are very large and have great balconies allowing views of the sea and sunsets. Ask for Norma or Nicholas Clewes, the owners. Norma said breakfast can be arranged with all sorts of "homesick" food. They just recently opened their restaurant/bar and it's been busy since the first day. They certainly make every effort to ensure the comfort of their guests.

> **Amenities:** *TV, a/c, mini-safe, mini-bar, restaurant/bar, beachfront.*
>
> **Good for:** *Couples, singles.*
>
> **Comment:** *This is one of the very few small hotels that face the ocean in this part of Tobago.*

TURTLE BEACH HOTEL, Courland Bay (mailing address: P.O. Box 201, Scarborough). ☎ 639-2851 or Fax 639-1495.

This hotel is right on the water and all beachfront rooms cost $140 single or double in high season (off-season rates fall to $112), plus tax and service charges. Children under 12 stay with you free of charge and will receive a discount in the restaurants. MAP is $45 per day. Other discounts may apply so be sure to ask. Sitting right on the beach, the grounds are a gardener's delight, planted with identified orchids and flowering tropical plants. The rooms are more spacious than at many island hotels and those on the second floor have steeply pitched wooden ceilings, which give even more space. There are 125 rooms, but the hotel appears deceptively smaller. Scuba diving and deep sea fishing are available at an additional charge. Their children's club is open Monday through Friday, offering supervised activities for children ages four to 12. The Turtle Beach, as you might have guessed, is a site for leatherback turtle nesting on the island. Hotel staff keep watch and will notify guests when a turtle is arriving. It's a great hotel for families. Some rooms have small separate sleeping quarters for a child at no extra charge. The air conditioners can be noisy. If you're looking for a resort-style hotel on the island, this would be one of our picks.

> **Amenities:** *Phone, a/c, restaurants, bar, nightly entertainment, beachfront, windsurfing, sunfish sailing, snorkeling, tennis, volleyball, business services, free children's club.*
>
> **Good for:** *Couples, families, just about anyone.*
>
> **Comment:** *Along with Arnos Vale, this is one of our favorites for location and appearance. The garden is beautiful and the beach is right there.*

Scarborough, Bacolet & The Atlantic Coast

OLD DONKEY CART HOUSE INN AND RESTAURANT, 73 Bacolet St., Scarborough, ☎ 639-3551 or Fax 639-6124.

Located on a hill overlooking Bacolet Point on Rockly Bay, the Donkey Cart has two small guest buildings with a total of 10 units and a pool in between. A quaint colonial home serves as office and restaurant. It is not on the water, but is well worth considering. Owned by Tobagonian Gloria and her German husband Reinhart Knapp, the hotel blends each of their influences beautifully. You'll see the mix reflected in the restaurant menu.

Rooms are $60 per person and the Presidential Suite is $300 for two, including tax and service charge. You'll save 20% in off-season. Although the rooms are delightful and spacious, I fell in love with the Presidential Suite. Wonderfully Caribbean and very romantic, the suite takes up the top floor of one of their two small buildings and is decorated with beautiful mahogany and has a pitched ceiling. Wooden louvers all around let in the constant breeze, so the lack of air conditioning should not be a problem except in the hottest weather. This is a Caribbean version of an artist's loft with very modern touches. Doors are all center hinged and swivel beautifully. The bed has white mosquito netting and a crocheted lace covering. There is a small fridge, a large shower – big enough for two – and a lovely bath. From the room-sized comfortably furnished porch you'll have a fantastic view of Scarborough and Bacolet Bay.

There's an attractive pool and satellite TV. They also have a villa to rent on Mt Irvine Golf Course at hole #7 (see *Houses to Rent*). You can discuss a meal plan with them when booking. MAP will be about $25 per person, plus tax and service charge. The restaurant offers a combination of local and international foods and is set in a lovely garden. Small lights in the trees give a romantic atmosphere.

Car rentals are available at discount. Make your reservations two months in advance for November through February. See the Old Donkey Cart listed under *Restaurants*. The Donkey Cart is an environmentally aware establishment with water recycling facilities. Non-smoking guest rooms are available.

> **Amenities:** *Small refrigerators, pool, restaurant/bar, water views, car rentals.*
>
> **Good for:** *Romantics.*
>
> **Comment:** *I love this place. For romantic couples it's perfect. Bacolet Beach is just two minutes away.*

PALM TREE VILLAGE (mailing address: P.O. Box 327, Little Rockly Bay, Milford). ☎ 639-4347/48/49 or Fax 639-4180.

The Palm Tree has 18 two-bedroom apartments and 20 guest rooms – all with telephone, satellite TV, and ocean views. In business for several years, they are now looking toward making time shares. Suites are large and comfortable with two bedrooms, living room, and full well-equipped kitchen. Each of the bedrooms has a bath and is air conditioned. One large patio is shared between two suites. Suites are $240 and rooms are $120. Out of season, a suite is $150 and rooms are $75. MAP is $35.

> **Amenities:** *Phone, TV, a/c, water view, pool, restaurant, bar, tennis courts, airport transfers, car rentals.*
>
> **Good for:** *Couples, families.*
>
> **Comment:** *For its average location, this hotel seems quite expensive. If you're determined to be near Scarborough, though, it's a good choice.*

RAWLE ARNASELEM'S GUEST HOUSE, Bacolet St., Bacolet. For information, call Mr. Rawle Arnaselem at ☎ 622-3359.

An older couple, Mr. and Mrs. Arnaselem rent two self-contained apartments for short-term stays. The rooms rent for under $10 per person, per night. He might put you in touch with Mrs. Roberts down the road if he doesn't have rooms available.

> **Amenities:** *Kitchenette.*
>
> **Good for:** *Couples or singles on a budget.*
>
> **Comment:** *This is a quiet area within walking distance of the beach. Rawle will give you a wealth of island information. He's a good story teller and a kind person.*

RESTRITE SEA GARDENS GUEST HOUSE, Delaford, ☎ 660-4220.

On the Atlantic coast, just off the Windward Road, this three-unit guest house is owned by the very gentle Mrs. Buntin Or. More of an apartment situation than an actual guest house, this is for folks on a tight budget who like things rustic. Rooms are on the beach with bath and kitchenette and cost $14, double. They are only about 12 feet from the water, depending on the tide. As you might guess from the price, it's not fancy. Gauguin probably would have liked it here and you might too, but you may want to stop by before committing yourself. The Restrite is for the more adventurous traveler who wants the beach and a taste of village life. The quality of the rooms is gradually improving and the beach is lovely.

> **Amenities:** *Kitchenette, beachfront.*
>
> **Good for:** *Couples or friends on a tight budget.*
>
> **Comment:** *This is for adventurous, budget-minded romantics.*

RICHMOND GREAT HOUSE INN, Belle Garden, ☎/Fax 660-4467.

This old estate residence has been carefully restored by Tobagonian Hollis Lynch, currently Professor of History at Columbia University. The inn sits on six acres in the hills 45 minutes from the airport in Crown Point and has a lovely remote feeling about it. It is just what one would dream up when imagining the perfect Caribbean guest house.

Filled with splendid African art and textiles, chess games, an eclectic library, and a great variety of walking sticks, the character of Richmond will charm and delight you. With a little luck, the professor will be in residence; he's thoroughly disarming.

The deluxe double at $110, the suite for two at $130, and the two-bedroom suite for two at $160 are the best accommodations. They are in the older part of the house and have a unique charm and fabulous views from oversized windows.

Richmond Great House Inn

Newer doubles are $85. These prices do not include the 10% room tax and 10% service charge. A meal plan with breakfast and dinner for two will add $35 to the price of a room. The food looked great. Summer season rates fall 10-15%. There is a pleasant pool just down from the reception area and tennis courts have just been completed.

> **Amenities:** *Fabulous views, antiques, pool, restaurant.*
>
> **Good for:** *Couples, singles, people who want a taste of the more gentle past, birdwatchers.*
>
> **Comment:** *The Richmond is an ideal place to stop for a night on your way to or from visiting Speyside and Charlotteville. It is a very peaceful base from which to hike in the hills or wend your way down the hillside to the quiet beach. If you can't stay, make it a must for lunch or dinner.*

STELLA "B" APARTMENTS, 79 Bacolet St., Bacolet, ☎ 639-5603.

Charming Eaulin Blondel has recently built two apartments as a part of her own home on the island. The house is delightfully Caribbean in appearance, white with perfectly matched blue and green trim. The studio apartments are very spacious and each has a porch overlooking Bacolet Bay. A path across the road leads down to the beach. Rooms are very reasonably priced at $25 single and $50 double, including tax and a Caribbean breakfast (a veritable feast of fresh fruits and more).

> **Amenities:** *TV, kitchenette, breakfast on Eaulin's terrace.*
> **Good for:** *Singles or couples who want a feeling of privacy in a pretty place close to the water.*
> **Comment:** *Eaulin is a warm and stylish a person, which is reflected in her home. We think this is one of the best guest houses on the island.*

Speyside, Charlotteville & Parlatuvier

BLUE WATERS INN, Batteaux Bay, Speyside, ☎ 660-4077 or 660-4341 and Fax 660-5195.

The setting for this hotel is spectacular, but the almost vertical road that reaches it gave me the willies and I strongly suggest that you have most of your meals there to avoid the drive. Blue Waters is owned by a couple of transplanted German ladies. Everything runs well and the service is excellent. Reginald MacLean, the General Manager, is very knowledgeable about the hotel business, but never loses sight of being a gracious host.

The hotel is wonderfully situated on its own private bay and lies sheltered by high hills on all sides. All of their 38 guest rooms face the beach and there is excellent diving and snorkeling.

Winter rates for standard rooms are $108 single and $121 double; in summer they run $70 single and $80 double. A one-bedroom suite/bungalow with kitchen, dining room, and porch is $275 in the winter and $150 in summer. These prices include tax and service. Meal plans are available; MAP is $31.37 and FAP is $38.46, all inclusive. Summer rates drop considerably with a standard room only $56 for two and $48 for one.

Most of the rooms are not air conditioned, but, with ceiling fans and wonderful ocean breezes, you won't need it. Book accommodations well in advance for high season. Be sure to ask for discounts if you're staying a week or more.

Amenities: *Beachfront, restaurant, bar, tennis courts, kayaks, windsurfing, snorkeling, and scuba diving.*
Good for: *Families, couples, scuba divers.*
Comment: *This is paradise for divers and most others enjoy its idyllic location.*

CHOLSON CHALETS, Charlotteville, ☎ 639-8553.

These six cottage apartments are economical at $25 single and $35 double per night. At the extreme northeastern tip of the island, Charlotteville is a small sleepy fishing village with no upscale tourist accommodations. These cottages are just fine for the relaxed tourist who wants a true Caribbean getaway and the chance to mingle with villagers on this small island. The apartments are managed by Miss Rosa, a very sweet and charming older lady. Her grandson seems to keep the details straight, but she does the cleaning and official renting. Book ahead if you're interested, because there's quite a waiting list. While we were there, all the other cottages were occupied by Danish families. For swimming, the lovely Pirate's Cove is just a walk over a steep hill. The whole town is pretty relaxed and is a good spot for fishing or scuba diving. Otherwise, good books, swimming, and snorkeling top the short list of things to do.

Amenities: *Waterfront, kitchenette.*
Good for: *Relaxed couples, friends, families.*
Comment: *Unfortunately, on a Saturday night noise from the bar next door continues to the wee hours. The look of the cottages is improving year to year.*

MAN-O-WAR BAY COTTAGES, Charlotteville, ☎ 660-4327 or Fax 660-4328.

Just outside the small village of Charlotteville, these several cottages are grouped among the trees at the edge of the beach. Each has a comfortable veranda, living/dining area, a separate fully-equipped kitchen and from one to four bedrooms. Equipped with ceiling and movable fans, but not air conditioned, they are designed to make use of sea breezes. A single is $55 and doubles are $60. A two-bedroom cottage for two is $70 and only $10 more with two more people. A three-bedroom is $95 and a four-bedroom is $140. These prices do not include tax of 15%. Arrangements can be made for maid service starting at $8/day for one or two persons and increasing with the size of your group. Cooks can be arranged for an additional fee. Charlotteville is about 36 miles from the airport and, surprisingly, this is one of the few places on the island that does not rent or make arrangements for car rentals. It would be best to take care of a rental before leaving Crown Point. Man-o-War Bay Cottages have been in existence long enough to have many repeat customers so you'll have to reserve months in advance. However, don't hesitate to give them a call on the spur of the moment in the hope of a cancellation.

> **Amenities:** *Beachfront, fully-equipped kitchens.*
> **Good for:** *Relaxed couples, families, friends, singles.*
> **Comment:** *If you are going to stay in Charlotteville, Man-o-War Bay Cottages is the best of what we found.*

MANTA LODGE, Windward Road, Speyside (mailing address: P.O. Box 433, Scarborough). ☎ 660-5268, Fax 660-5030, or toll-free in the US, ☎ (800) 544-7631.

Just opened in 1995, the 22-room Manta Lodge has all the spit and polish of a new hotel. It is small and offers personal service and a professional dive shop. In fact, the owner, Sean Robinson, is himself a divemaster. Standard rooms are $80 single in winter and $65 in summer; doubles are $90, lowering to $75 in summer. Make sure to ask for a standard with balcony. Superior rooms are $95 in winter and $80 in summer. Doubles are $105 in winter and $90 in summer. Loft rooms cost $150 double in winter and $125 in summer. Rates do not include 10% tax and 10% service charge. Meals plans are available at $30 MAP and $45 FAP, plus 15% tax and 10% service.

Most guests are serious divers, but all guests are entitled to a free scuba experience and novices often sign up for further training. We preferred the standard rooms which have ceiling fans, but not a/c, or the superior rooms with a/c; with a few exceptions they all have wonderful balconies overlooking the bay. Loft rooms were a good idea, but the execution just wasn't there.

> **Amenities:** *Quiet a/c, phone, pool, restaurant/bar, dive shop.*
> **Good for:** *Couples, friends, scuba divers.*
> **Comment:** *Manta is a very appealing small hotel, one of three in Speyside. It is perfect for anyone with a serious interest in diving. For those who don't yet know how to dive, try it here; you might just be seduced.*

PARLATUVIER TOURIST RESORT, Parlatuvier, ☎ 639-5629.

Just one minute from the beach, this small basic hotel has five units, with a variety of options: bath/shared bath, kitchen/shared kitchen. Owned by Duran Chance and his wife Islin, the hotel's rooms are $25, all inclusive. There's no maid service, but the building is new and well maintained. It is located on one of the more beautiful bays on the island – Parlatuvier. There is nothing to do in this tiny town, but enjoy the sun, sand, and water. It is very quiet and used to be visually gorgeous until they constructed a concrete fishing pier in the middle of the bay. The Chances also own the general store in town, next door to the apartments. Right from your balcony you can people-watch.

> **Amenities:** *Some a/c rooms, kitchenettes, grocery store.*
> **Good for:** *Couples, friends on a budget.*
> **Comment:** *Good for a taste of village life in the Caribbean. Okay for the price.*

SPEYSIDE INN, Windward Road, Speyside, ☎ 660-4852.

This pretty hotel with just six rooms and one studio overlooks Tyrell's Bay, where you will have a view across to Little Tobago Island (see *Sights to See*). There is not much action in Speyside that does not involve the ocean. It is considered the best area for diving and snorkeling in Tobago and there are lots of full-time fishermen in the small town of Charlotteville just over the hill. Singles here are $75 in high season, $60 in low; doubles are $85 in high and $70 in low. A room tax of 10% will be added to your bill. These rates include breakfast. If you're not a guest of the hotel, breakfast is $6 and lunch/dinner can be had for about $20, not including tax and service. All rooms face the ocean and each has a balcony.

> **Amenities:** *Beachfront, restaurant, good views.*
> **Good for:** *Couples, friends, scuba divers.*
> **Comment:** *This is a very pretty small hotel.*

Houses For Rent

MOT MOT RIDGE, home of David and Hillary Montgomery in Arnos Vale, ☎ 639-1931 (in Tobago).

This lovely home rents for $1,925 a week in high season and $1,050 in low. They'll rebate the 15% agent fee included in these prices if you rent directly through them. David and Hillary are gracious Trinidadians who spent an afternoon showing us their home and talking about what went into selecting the land and building plans. Constructed three years ago, the house sits very high on a hill overlooking the ocean on one side and grassy hills on the other. They spared no time, effort, or expense building this colonial-style Caribbean residence.

The house is wonderfully open and carefully furnished to create casual, comfortable, elegant spaces. Upstairs you'll find three air-conditioned bedrooms and two baths. All rooms have spectacular views and access to the second floor porch. Downstairs there's a living/dining room, a cook's dream kitchen, and laundry room. There's a caretaker who lives in a small cottage on the grounds and a maid will clean twice weekly.

Beside the house is a small immaculate pool. A 10-minute walk down a path in front of the house will lead you to a very private beach. It has no access by road. The walk uphill will take a bit more time, but there is always a price for privacy. Contact David at: D. Montgomery & Co., Chartered Accts., 118 Abercromby St., Port of Spain, Trinidad, ☎ 623-4573 or Fax 623-6610. Their home phone number is ☎ 624-5445.

Mot Mot House for rent

PLANTATION BEACH VILLAS, ☎ 639-0455.

These charming Caribbean gingerbread houses have become architectural models for the island. The six identical houses are set on a lushly gardened hill overlooking Stone Haven Bay. Each has three air-conditioned bedrooms (two upstairs), each with a private bath. Downstairs there's a comfortable and attractive living/dining area, plus a complete kitchen. All rooms open onto spacious covered verandas with deck furniture. There's a barbecue grill, a wall safe, and laundry room.

Daily maid and laundry service are included. Cooks and babysitters are available at a small additional charge. Rental during the high season, December 16 through April 15, is $450 per day for four persons or $510 for six. Long-term and group rates are negotiable. Low season rates fall to about $300.

Reservations should be made as early as possible, at least three to four months in advance. Repeat visitors receive a 15% discount on their stay. Although each of the houses is independent and private, there are opportunities for socializing at the shared pool and bar. Bryan Akien, the manager, and his assistant will do everything to make your stay comfortable, from arranging car rentals to tours of the island. Of the six houses, only number four lacks a sea view. It is surrounded by trees. *Special Note:* These houses are located just above Grafton Beach, where the leatherback turtles begin to lay their eggs in late April.

Plantation Villas

VILLA GREEN SEVEN, owned by Gloria and Reinhart Knapp.

This very beautifully designed, modern, luxurious home is set on the grounds of the Mt. Irvine Hotel. For information and reservations, contact Sherwin Peterson, manager of the Old Donkey Cart Inn, ☎ 639-3551. Costing $2,000 a week, the house has three living rooms, three bedrooms, a reading and TV room, a dining area and two kitchens, three baths, and a pool. Nearby you'll find an 18-hole golf course and flood-lit tennis courts. The beach is a short walk away.

Camping

Camping is not common on the island, but we did run into a young couple camping by themselves at Englishman's Bay. Avid snorkelers, they were catching their dinners daily and having a wonderful time. Local police checked on them each afternoon to make sure they were okay. While it seems idyllic, we realize that this might not be a great choice for everyone. Although Tobago is a relatively safe environment, we'd recommend starting your trip at Canoe Bay Beach Park.

The T & T government is planning to develop camping facilities in the Bloody Bay area at the end of the road on the Caribbean side of the island, but nothing is in place yet.

CANOE BAY BEACH PARK, Canaan near Shirvan Road.

A beach, camping, and picnic area, Canoe Bay is private. It has a wonderful beach and large grassy areas with palapas for island getaways and parties. Palapas are open-sided shelters with palm-leaf roofs that offer protection from rain or hot sun. The park also has modest camping facilities. You'll have your choice of where to pitch your tent, clean tile bathrooms, and shower facilities. Showers are open-air, similar to those at beaches to wash off salt and sand. It is a very pleasant quiet place with a wide sandy beach. The water is blue-green, calm, and shallow for quite a distance, making this a great place to bring children. There's a bar open daily till 5 PM, when the park closes. It seemed a perfect place for a country getaway. The cost of a campsite is $5 per person; groups of 10 or more receive a discount. Sleeping units are planned for the future, but there's no date for completion in mind. Winston Baptiste is the manager and he's delightful, answering all your questions with a smile. The owners are Tobagonians. While used mainly for parties and weddings, Canoe Bay is also home to a Jazz Festival in October. There are no phones and no electricity at the site itself, but you can make reservations through the James Almandoz Real Estate office at ☎ 639-3691 or 639-2631. If you're camping they'll lock up valuables for you and have someone on site all the time. More activities are planned for the future, including tennis and a kid's playground.

Food

Unlike many Caribbean islands, Tobago has fruit and vegetable farms and ranches raising cows, sheep, and goats. Fresh fish, lobster, and conch are also readily available.

Surprisingly, the lower down on the restaurant food chain you go, the better the fare gets. Local food is delicious – mixes of stews, vegetables, fish with light touches of herbs. Generally, if you select local dishes on any menu, you can't go wrong.

Because Tobago is becoming more of a tourist destination, new restaurants are opening all the time. We've listed some of the better places we found, but there seems to be a new one every week.

Cooking For Yourself

Many smaller guest houses and hotels on the island provide cooking facilities. If you want to cook while on vacation, here are some places to get started.

Fruits and vegetables are available all over the island at small roadside stalls. Tomatoes and lettuce and peppers and onions and plantains and papayas and mangoes and pineapples and watermelons and bananas and lemons and limes...

The Golden Grove Farm in Canaan raises livestock and ages their own meat. Unfortunately, most of it is frozen for sale, but they'll sell you fresh if you catch them at the right time. Frozen meats, fancy groceries, fresh heavy cream, and interesting cheeses are available at **Moshead's**, just off Shirvan Road near Starting Gate.

Vegetables at the Scarborough Market

A food fancier's real highlight is the **weekly market** in Scarborough on Saturday morning, where you can buy very fresh foods of all kinds. The meat market is inside the main building, where you'll find beef, lamb, pork, goat and some body parts you'd rather not see. Free-range eggs and chickens are also available. Outside in the market, fruitarians and vegetarians will have a field day. Everything looks and tastes delicious. You won't find any of those US supermarket mystery foods, like big bright red strawberries that taste like air. Beans and salt and oils, crabs and herbs, vegetables and fruits are in abundance. It's a celebration not to be missed.

Penny Savers Supermarket in Canaan, just outside of Crown Point, has all the basics you'll need – food staples, beers and liquors, but no fruits or vegetables. They have lots of candy bars and some other home-away-from-home foods for the homesick traveler. The **Francis Supermarket** beside the Crown Point Hotel is much smaller than Penny Savers, but is within walking distance of hotels in Crown Point. Out in front of the market there's a great fruit and vegetable fellow selling produce from his truck. He squeezes the sweetest orange juice for you right there.

Fish

In Crown Point, fishermen come in with their catch by the **Conrado Hotel** on Pigeon Point. You can show up there by the fishing shacks at about 3 PM and see what's available. The catch will vary by season,

Fish cleaning station, Pigeon Point

but you may find flying fish, dolphin (the fish), red snapper, or grouper. You may also enjoy seeing a seine (a large net used to trap fish) being pulled at Mt. Irvine, Black Rock, Turtle Beach, Bloody Bay, Man-o-War Bay or Castara. On **King's Bay Beach** between 1 and 4 in the afternoon you can buy the morning's catch, which might be yellow or black fin tuna, kingfish, dolphin fish, snapper or grouper. The two young fishermen, Stephen and Hosford, will filet it. If you are staying at the eastern end of the island, **Charlotteville** is the place for fish.

In Crown Point one day, while awaiting the return of the fishermen, a diver arrived with several buckets of lobsters. We bought two big ones and found two great guys, Bonzo and Nubia, to cook them in a big pot over an open fire. As we waited, they gave us treats from the grill, yellow fin tuna and flying fish, to tide us over till the lobster was ready. Tobago has some really nice people. If you are buying lobsters the best people to see are Cuthbert Williams or Renwick Thom (☎ 639-9425) at Pigeon Point. If you are at all inclined to cook, don't miss the lobster and dolphin fish.

Lobster fisherman, Cuthbert

Beer & Rum

Local beers are **Carib** and **Stag**. Either might be the next Red Stripe. You may also get a chance to try **bush rum**, a local brew that's as good as it is powerful. Rum is made in Trinidad so you'll be offered lots of rum and cokes and rum punches.

Vegetarians

For vegetarians, Tobago offers fresh fruits and vegetables galore, but restaurant offerings are limited. If you eat fish, there's no problem. If not, the **Turtle Beach Hotel** specializes in vegetarian menus, but it's fairly expensive. Lots of small local food stalls offer non-meat *rotis* that our vegetarian friends thought very good. In Scarborough, there are three vegetarian shops in the mall, but none have extensive menus. **E & F Health Foods** is probably the best for herbs. **Penny Savers** carries various forms of vegetable protein and soy products.

Reservations

You'll see lots of places requesting reservations. It's rare that a restaurant is full, but reservations give them an idea of how many people are coming and how much to cook. In many restaurants, we showed up without booking ahead and were the only ones there. Don't hesitate to stop by without calling ahead.

Treats

Sesame candy sweets are available at the airport from a number of friendly ladies. The sweets come in all sorts of shapes and are pretty good. For candy bar lovers there's a good supply at **Penny Savers**.

Restaurants

Crown Point

ELEVEN DEGREES NORTH, Store Bay Road off Pigeon Point Road, Crown Point, ☎ 639-0996.

This is the first crowded restaurant we've seen and that's got to be an indication of things being done right. Owned by Bechna Seereeram and Barry Treau, it is a new, nicely designed open-air place on the way to Pigeon Point. The wood ceiling, delicate pastels, individually painted tables, and revolving exhibitions of local art make a sophisticated setting. Open for dinner at 6:30 PM and closed Sunday and Monday, they have a reggae duo entertaining on Wednesdays and acoustic live music when it can be arranged. The night we were there they had a talented guitarist. A lobster crêpe appetizer at $6 followed by an entrée of homemade carrot and spinach pasta with chicken or lobster sauce at $17 should leave you too full for a slice of guava cheesecake, but do your best. Dinner with wine costs about $80 for two.

ALFRED'S BARBECUE, Store Bay Beach, Crown Point. Usually open only two days a week.

Alfred is a tall serious man we met over by Miss Esmie's beach stall while having lunch. He's there most days selling tickets for his barbecues, or you may see him on the beach where he rents chairs and umbrellas. His barbecue menu gives you a choice of chicken, fish, or lobster. The price is a little high, but the food was some of the best we had on the island. The kingfish was perfectly prepared, as were the vegetables, rice and salad. It's a very romantic setting on the beach with lanterns flaming on the sand and a steel band playing. Usually 20 to 30 people attend and five or six fellows cook and serve. Dinner is all-inclusive with drinks and costs between $22 and $35 per person. Alfred's barbecues are on the beach at Store Bay at 8 PM.

COLUMBUS SNACK BAR, Store Bay Road, with a DuMaurier Cigarettes awning, Crown Point. No telephone.

Owned by Mervin and Teresa Alfred, this small restaurant is a real find for delicious basic food at a good price. They're open seven days a week from 6:30 AM to 12 or 1 AM, serving breakfast, lunch, and dinner. On Fridays they have a barbecue with chicken, pork, or fish starting at 7 PM. Food is simple, but all of it is freshly prepared and tasty. You can eat inside, but there are also tables with palm shading outside. Teresa is 6 feet 4 inches tall and can she cook! I'd recommend the fried chicken. Chicken dinners for two with drinks will cost under $15.

DELI BERI, Corner Store Bay and Pigeon Point Roads, Crown Point, ☎ 639-4322.

This bright new place offers ice cream, desserts (we liked the double chocolate cake), fresh bread, croissants, and pizza. Open from 10 AM to 10 PM.

IN SEINE SEAFOOD RESTAURANT, beside the Tropikist Hotel, Crown Point, ☎ 639-9347/9467.

Specializing in seafood, In Seine is a pleasant open-air restaurant set on the lawn next to the Tropikist Hotel. Dinner runs about $30 for two with drinks. Our meals of fish and shrimp were well prepared and attractively presented. Although we didn't indulge, the desserts looked good – lots of ice creams – and all were served with sparklers, a fun surprise. They are congenial people and the service is good.

MISS JEAN'S/MISS ESMIE'S, Store Bay Beach, Crown Point.

Two very popular folksy places to eat on the cheap, these small kiosks across from Store Bay Beach are run by island ladies who make filling T & T food at great prices. I'd especially recommend the beef stew at Miss Esmie's. Right there as well is a bar/restaurant, where they make a passable hamburger with fries.

Two people can feed themselves for under $10.

TOUCAN INN AND BONKERS, Store Bay Road, Crown Point, ☎ 639-7173.

British owners, Chris James and James Vaughan, opened this teak extravaganza in 1995. Constructed as an open-air bar/restaurant, the heavy teak lends it a substantial feel. Food is reasonably priced. Bonkers has developed quite a following of vacationing Trinidadians. It can be warm even in the evening; you'll be more comfortable wearing very light clothes.

TROPIKIST HOTEL RESTAURANT, Crown Point, ☎ 639-8512/3.

This restaurant can't be seen from the road, but inside you'll find a pretty open-air setting by the pool. With cloth-covered tables and a view of moonlit Store Bay, it's hard to go wrong. You can take a look at their daily menu board in the reception office or by the side of the road. They are open to special requests; their curries are worth a try. Dinner for two with drinks will cost about $35.

Mid-Caribbean Coast

ARNOS VALE HOTEL, Arnos Vale Road, Arnos Vale, ☎ 639-2881/82.

For a big splurge, try an Italian dining experience at the Arnos Vale. Bring your appetite; it's quite something. See details under the Arnos Vale Hotel listing.

BLACK ROCK CAFE, Black Rock, ☎ 639-7625.

Open-air dining with linens, lots of breezy air, and ceiling fans to keep it moving. This restaurant is owned by a BWIA pilot and offers a varied menu written on a large chalk board. Open from noon to 3 PM for lunch and 6 PM till the last customer leaves for dinner. Two of us had lunch and drinks for under $20. The food is appealingly presented.

THE PEACOCK MILL, Friendship Estate, Canaan, ☎ 639-0503.

Take the dirt road across the street from Azard's Tyre Shop on Milford Road in Canaan. Go down about a third of a mile and you'll see the restaurant ahead on the left. It's a white building with a huge tree in the front yard, which is home to 20 or so peacocks. Lunch is served from noon to 3 PM and dinner from 6 to 10:30 PM, but they're not rigid about hours. Opened just this past year by a British family, the restaurant serves a varied and more complex menu than is common on the island. Entrées begin at about $13 and go up from there. The lunchtime chef, Nigel Williams, is great with grilled fish, which couldn't have tasted better. A simple lunch for two with drinks runs $30 with everything included. Aaron Woods is the evening chef. On Saturday nights they have a popular barbecue and party which can last till dawn. This year they've added an outdoor palm-covered area with a pool table. It should be a great spot for an evening of liming with friends.

SEA HORSE INN, Old Grafton Road, Black Rock, ☎ 639-0686 (also see a hotel listing).

This restaurant was opened in 1995 by owner/managers Norma and Nicholas. Specializing in foods prepared in an international style that you'll be right at home with, it looks as though they have a success. The restaurant is just below the Grafton Hotel, across from the palm-lined beach. Its modern decor is stylish and sophisticated. The menu is varied, with appetizers from $3 to $6, and seafood and beef entrées from $12 to $25. They're open for lunch from 12 to 3 PM and dinner from 7 PM. Godwin Taylor is the chef. Best to make reservations.

LA TARTARUGA RESTAURANT, Buccoo Bay, ☎ 639-0940.

Tartaruga is owned by an Italian who puts a genuine touch from his homeland on all of the dishes. He even makes all of the fresh pasta himself. Everyone on the island thinks highly of La Tartaruga. It's a little on the expensive side – dinner for two costs in the region of $60. Open evenings; closed Sunday and Monday.

Scarborough & Bacolet

BLUE CRAB, Main & Robinson Sts., Scarborough, ☎ 639-2737.

Serving local and international dishes at about $8 for lunch and $12 for dinner, the Blue Crab is a good choice. The restaurant itself is attractive and it has great views. It would make a good stop on your way back from Fort St. George. Reservations required.

OLD DONKEY CART HOUSE RESTAURANT AND WINE BISTRO, Bacolet St., Bacolet, ☎ 639-3551.

Local and international cuisine is served in a lovely setting outside a French colonial style house and the owner specializes in German wines. Candlelight on the table and twinkling lights strung in the trees overhead make a very romantic setting. We dined there on our anniversary and were very happy with our meal, the service, and the setting. Dinner for two with cocktails was under $50, including tax and tip.

Tobago Restaurants

ROUSELLES, Old Windward Road, Bacolet, ☎ 639-4738.

Casual, but sophisticated, Rouselles is open for dinner only, and from 3 to 11 PM for cocktails. This five-year-old restaurant is owned by Bobbie Evans and Charlene Goodman. With a lovely view, wood floors, teak tables, and lots of plants, the outside porch has the best seating. Inside is also pleasant, with a teak bar and relaxed, but elegant ambiance. They have four entrées – lobster, seafood, pork chops, and chicken – all beautifully prepared. Meals cost between $15 and $30, plus drinks. The porch overlooks a pretty garden for those who tire of the sea view, and music plays in the background. Reservations for a table on the porch are necessary during the high season.

Atlantic Coast

RICHMOND GREAT HOUSE INN, Belle Garden, ☎ 660-4467.

This is your very best choice on the drive from Scarborough to Speyside for a delicious and freshly prepared lunch or dinner. There just isn't another place like it. The inn sits in the hills and has spectacular views all the way to the ocean in the distance. You must call ahead and make reservations for dinner. This four-course meal is enjoyed from 6:30 to 8 PM and costs $50 for two. Dinner is always served in the main house dining room, but lunch may also be served in the small open-air dining area on the lawn. A full lunch with dessert will be about $20 for two.

Speyside & Charlotteville

GAIL'S CAFE, Charlotteville. (No phone, but you can stand anywhere in town and shout!)

This is the place in town for a breakfast of pancakes or omelettes with fresh local juices and homemade bread. They're also open for dinner and for $6 you can enjoy their curried crab and dumplings or other local specialties. They have a few outside tables so you can feel the cool of the evening while eating.

JEMMA'S TREE HOUSE RESTAURANT, Speyside, ☎ 660-4066.

Jemma's, as the name implies, sits in a tree over the water. Its unique charm would hold up nicely to competition from other restaurants if it had to, but there are few other choices in Speyside. You'll find no printed menu, but chicken, fish, or shrimp dishes are served with rice, fried plantains, vegetables and salad. They do not serve any alcoholic beverages, but you are quite welcome to bring your own. Three of us ate lunch at this island institution for $32, including tip. It looks like Jemma's is getting more expensive, but eating in a tree house seems worth it. The food is not fancy, but it is nicely presented and the servings are plentiful.

Things To See & Do

Evenings

CABIN PUB, Carrington St., Scarborough, ☎ 639-3196.
This is a place where the yachty crowd hangs out when in Scarborough. They have wonderful fresh juices made by Eve Mendez, who owns the Gingerbread guest house in Plymouth (see the *Tobago Accommodations*).

CRYSTAL PALACE, Milford Road, Scarborough, ☎ 639-4829.
This is a small casino reminiscent of the speakeasies of the prohibition era. They have blackjack, poker, baccarat, and will have craps as soon as the table arrives. We met a great dealer there named Ginine. Unfortunately, she was there only a short time to train staff and has now returned to Trinidad to work in a casino. Crystal Palace is in Scarborough and is open from 6 PM onward Tuesday through Sunday evenings. Men must wear long pants. Table limits are TT$10 or about $1.75. These may change a bit, but it is still pretty inexpensive gambling. For avid blackjack players, they have a favorable rule – you can double down at any time. *Note:* It's the first casino we've ever come across that charges for drinks.

GOLDEN STAR, Crown Point, ☎ 639-0873.
Open seven days a week from 7 AM for dining, but better known for music and dancing till the wee hours. They have a special entertainment night on Wednesdays, but call to check. You'll find it next to the Surfside Inn in Crown Point where the road divides to go to Pigeon Point.

LES COTEAUX CULTURAL THEATER
Choreographer Verleen Bobb-Lewis been has working with this 22-member troupe of dancers and musicians since February 1988. You can see them perform at the Crown Point Hotel Sundays, Turtle

Beach Hotel Wednesday, Mt. Irvine Hotel on Thursday and The Grafton Hotel on Saturday. Call the hotels ahead to verify any changes in the schedule. They're *great*, offering spectacular, exciting entertainment. Write to Verleen at Cradley Trace, Government House Road, Scarborough, Tobago.

OLD DONKEY CART INN, 73 Bacolet St., Bacolet, ☎ 639-3551.

This romantic inn has entertainment and dancing under the stars on Friday and Saturday evenings. See also listings under *Restaurants* and *Accommodations*.

PEACOCK MILL, Friendship Estate, Canaan, ☎ 639-0503.

Also listed under *Restaurants*, the Peacock Mill now has a palm-covered area outside with a pool table. It's a pleasant place to play pool with friends and have a drink or two. Watch for special weekend parties.

PLEASURE PIRATES

This is a performance group recommended by Verleen Bobb-Lewis, choreographer of the Les Coteaux Cultural Theater. We didn't get a chance to see them perform, but we were so impressed by Verleen's other work, we'll take her word for their abilities.

STARTING GATE, Shirvan Road, ☎ 639-0225.

Starting Gate is a bar/pool hall with dancing till dawn. The music can get pretty noisy after 11 PM. Its name comes from an old race course that used to lie in the fields next door. It is getting rowdier these days and women should definitely not show up alone.

SUNDAY SCHOOL, Buccoo.

This Sunday evening block party at Buccoo is an institution on the island. Drinking, dancing, and socializing start around 10 PM Sunday evening and go till dawn. It's a great way for young people to meet and interact on this quiet island. There is recorded music and drinks are available at either of two bars. Hundreds of folks attend and about 10% are tourists. Beers cost $1 or you can bring rum and order cokes to make your own drinks. It's best to go in couples or groups. Single women may get more attention than they want. Parking can be a problem; consider using a taxi. It will cost you about $15 to have the taxi drop you there and return for you when you are ready to leave.

Miscellaneous

Chess

Store Bay Beach, Crown Point

A fellow named Bryan plays chess on the road above Store Bay Beach. You'll find him most days in any one of the small craft stalls. He's always set for a game. Chess aficionados can make there way there and pick up a game. Everyone will have a word or two on the progress of the game. It makes a lovely diversion and is a nice way to get to know folks from the island.

Pulling A Seine

On Turtle Beach and a few other beaches you'll still be able to see this cooperative fishing effort. A huge net is cast from shore early in the morning and later pulled in, hand-over-hand, by village fishermen and whoever else is there to help. If you pitch in, you'll get a share of the catch. See page 144.

Shell Shopping

Whole days can be passed idly searching the beaches for the flotsam of the sea – pieces of coral and great shells are everywhere. You can also buy large shells at the small stalls by Store Bay Beach, but it's more fun to hunt for them yourself. You'll run into trouble with US Customs if you buy any exotic coral or turtle products that are sometimes for sale. Many of these pieces are endangered species and you should avoid promoting this unlawful business.

Soccer

On Sundays there is often a 2-on-2 pick up game on the wide lawn at the Tropikist Hotel in Crown Point.

Sights

Note: For any of the hikes or birdwatching trails, you'll need good walking shoes. Binoculars and cameras are also a must. Tobago has a much tamer environment than Trinidad.

Roxborough

Argyle Waterfall

Official hours are from 8 AM to 3 PM, but they are flexible. The entrance and parking fees also seem to vary. Expect to pay $1 per person or up to $5 per car. We entered without a guide and no one objected, but other visitors were turned away for not having one. A guide is not really needed unless you're going to climb the waterfall. To avoid paying an exorbitant rate for a guide at the site, visit Argyle with your own hired guide.

As you're walking in to this beautiful waterfall, you'll pass by a swampy area on your right and, if you're lucky, you'll be there when the white and pale blue water lilies are in bloom. There are even some ramshackle picnic tables, where you can rest and enjoy the glorious view on this relatively short walk. Birds and butterflies abound even if nothing's blooming.

There's a guest house on the grounds that has two units, each with kitchen, bath, and bedroom. Set in the middle of nowhere, it might make a lovely hideaway. Unfortunately it was closed during our visit and no one was able to give us any information. Along the walk are banana trees and flamboyant trees with orange flowers. Flamboyants are often home to the king of the woods bird, whose nests are long sack-like bags resembling burlap.

You'll be getting close to the falls when you first come upon a creek. Follow it along the rocks and you'll arrive in a few minutes. The falls run year round, but are more spectacular in the rainy season. Have a swim or climb to the top for a water massage. I'd only recommend this to those who really like climbing. I stayed below and entertained myself with swimming, admiring the falls, and chit-chatting with a fellow named Bashumba, maker and purveyor of handcrafted leather and bead work.

Cocoa Estate

This isn't noted on the tourist trail, but we found it interesting – especially for chocolate lovers. It is in Roxborough and you'll drive right through the old cocoa estates if you are heading to Argyle Waterfall from town.

You'll see acres of 20- or 30-foot trees with six-inch pods ranging from purple to yellow to red hanging off woody sections. The yellow cocoa pods are harvested, dried, and ground into chocolate. If you get one that's bright yellow, crack it open and eat the white gooey stuff inside (you'll have to spit out the seeds). It doesn't taste like chocolate, but has a delicate sweet flavor. When picking pods, watch for the cocoa snakes which live in the trees and are called Cocoa Police by the locals. They aren't poisonous, but you may be startled. As you enter the estate you'll see a ruined stone building where slaves worked. The building is being slowly restored.

Scarborough

Scarborough is a ramshackle market and commercial port town. Be wary of taxi fares here; always confirm the fare before setting off. Saturday is market day in Scarborough; don't miss it!

Botanical Gardens

Worth a visit if you are in Scarborough. No entrance fee.

Fort King George

Built by the English in the late 1770's, this old fort is a wonderful sight with spectacular views at sunset. There are several colonial buildings, cannon, and two museums. One has memorabilia of the island, both Amerindian and Colonial, and the other has recent island paintings and sculpture.

The grounds are beautiful and well maintained. Admission is free, except to the artifact museum where they charge $1. There are wonderful plants all over the grounds and some magnificent trees covered in epiphytes. The Tobago hospital is right next door.

Speyside

A very pretty quiet village on the eastern end of the island. Offshore is Little Tobago. This is a diver's heaven.

When we stopped by the Mt. Irvine Watersports shop one afternoon we met Bertrand Bhikarry, the owner. We were talking about our writing of this book and he contributed the following essay on pulling seines.

"Seine Time, Same Place"

By Bertrand Bhikarry

"Don't stand there when it's coming in," the old man advised, "you never know what could be swimming around in that net." The woman back-peddles away, her eyes wide with anticipation. She continues to jockey for a position, however, between the villagers hauling in the net, and her friends, who are trying to capture the entire event on their video camera. Except for the nationality of the onlookers, this scene has remained remarkably unchanged on Tobago's beaches for close to one hundred and fifty years.

Each time the fishermen bring in the seine, people congregate at the water's edge, baskets and pails dangling from their hands, while onlookers stare and village dogs dash around, eager to snatch at a morsel.

As the bunt of the net comes in, fishermen, standing by in their pirogues, skim off bait fish and tenderly deposit them in bait wells. These small fish will become the bait for the next day's catch. As the net is drawn in, prized fishes – the kingfish, dolphin, and tuna – begin to appear and are snapped up eagerly by the anxious fishermen. Once the main catch has been retrieved, the net is hauled further out of the water, just beyond the surf, and the remaining fish are dumped into depressions scooped out in the sand.

Next, the owner, or one of his trusted assistants, allots portions of the catch to awaiting housewives, laborers, and market vendors. Any money collected goes under his hat, hidden high and dry, but not everyone pays in cash.

Onlookers might wonder, how does this activity remain viable, when most of the time, not a lot of fish are caught. What holds such a large group of men together in so consistent a manner?

Usually the equipment belongs to one person, a resident of the village who has acquired the lump sum necessary to purchase a net and the boat used to set it out. He or she in turn hires a core group of about six to 10 men. Their job is to set out and haul in the net, and perform any necessary repairs. They are paid weekly, an amount proportionate to sales from the fish they have caught. Nets are set in the morning, and hauled in immediately afterwards. If a shoal of fish is evident in the bay, the men may repeat the 'shoot' later in the day. They work, on average, six days a week, with public holidays, village harvest festivals, and fishermen's fetes considered 'rest' days.

The number of nets used on any one beach is dictated by the size of the bay and the population of the village. The types of fish caught range from bait fishes, the herring, balao, and jacks, to the larger species, such as bonito, kingfish, salmon, and sometimes small shark.

At present, beaches that can boast of decent seine fishing activity are those at Mount Irvine Bay, Black Rock, Turtle Beach, Castara, Bloody Bay, Man-o-War Bay, and, on the windward side of the island, Mount St. George and Goodwood. This little industry provides direct employment for close to 300 people, and creates economic opportunities for 50 fish market vendors and 40 deep sea fishermen.

The bad news for people dependent on this type of fishery is that the industry's days are numbered. A declining catch rate and a lack of interest from the younger men mean that one of Tobago's signature activities will become a thing of the past. A beautiful memory, poignantly recorded by our visitors video cameras.

Little Tobago Island Preserve

Little Tobago is also known as Paradise Island because in 1909 Sir William Ingram, an estate owner on Tobago, released 24 pairs of endangered greater birds of paradise there. Lying a mile or so off the coast at Speyside, Little Tobago is now home to a number of species, but the bird of paradise has not been seen there in over a decade.

Resident birds, including feral chickens and red-billed tropic birds, can be seen, and the redfooted and brown boobies make temporary homes on the island. It's not an unpleasant trip and birdwatchers may find it to be quite exciting. Try your best to find a legitimate guide service, perhaps David Rooks (☎ 639-3325). Finding someone in Speyside with a boat will limit your potential to appreciate the island.

Murchison Trace
Just before Speyside

If you are visiting the eastern end of the island you might want to take a long leisurely walk through these woods, where you'll see lots of birds and plants native to Tobago. To find it, watch for the dirt road off to the left just before the Speyside lookout. Tobago offers many opportunities for hiking through the woods and this is one of the better paths.

Elsewhere On The Island

Buccoo Reef

This once pristine reef lies off Pigeon Point. Tragically, parts of it have suffered from a combination of pollution, boat anchoring, and

Tobago Sights

unmindful tourism. The best way to see the reef is by scuba diving or snorkeling. Arrangements can be made with any of the dive shops in Crown Point or with Mt. Irvine Watersports.

Glass bottom boats also ply their way to Buccoo Reef on a daily basis from various spots on the island. The round trip to the reef takes about 2½ hours and costs $10 per person. The ride out to the reef is pleasant enough. On arrival, an anchor is thrown overboard and dragged until it catches on the coral, a thoughtless and environmentally damaging act that kills not only coral, but the many, many lifeforms that exist therein. Protective shoes are passed out so that passengers may walk on the reef, destroying it further, which at this point is only three feet under the boat. We stayed on board and looked through the glass bottom at the mostly dead coral below.

Once everyone is back on board, the anchor is dragged up and the boat motors over what is called the **Coral Garden**. This area is too deep for anyone to trample on, and so remains a fantastic sight. The next stop is locally called the **Nylon Pool**. This area of the reef is very shallow, feeling as warm as a bath to the feet, with a coral sand bottom. They say if you swim in the Nylon Pool you'll feel 10 years younger. With the rum and cokes and beers that have been consumed on board, I'm sure this stop does make a lot of people feel younger. Buccoo is stunning where it is still alive.

St. Giles Island
Off the northeast shore of Tobago

This is a rocky island known for nesting birds not far from Little Tobago. It has little substantial vegetation and reminds me of some of the barren islands in the Galapagos, where so many birds nest happily in rocky crags.

Adventure Farm & Nature Reserve
Arnos Vale Road, Arnos Vale, ☎ 639-2839

This is a tropical organic farm with many varieties of fruits, sheep and racing goats. Two acres have been left undeveloped as habitat for local birds, which include king of the woods, chachalaca, woodpeckers, herons, egrets, parakeets, blue tanagers, hummingbirds, bare-eyed thrush, jacamar, and barred antshrike. Open Monday to Friday 7 AM to 5:45 PM.

Charlotteville

The largest village in Tobago, Charlotteville sits on a small bay surrounded by mountains. It is undeveloped and quite beautiful.

There are a few rustic places to stay. The town faces the harbor and its anchored fishing boats. Each evening offers a fabulous sunset. We arrived in Charlotteville in the late afternoon and, at first, local residents seemed reserved. Once we'd settled in at one of the Cholson Cottages on the main road, everyone accepted us and were very friendly.

Crusoe's Cave, Crown Point

Tobago has the honor of being the island chosen most likely to have provided a safe haven for the fictional Robinson Crusoe. There is a small cave where he is said to have lived and you can see it by paying the small fee of about $1 to a lovely woman named Alison or her mother Mrs. Crooks. They own the right of way to the shore where the cave is found and maintain the rough stairs that lead to it.

We decided to bike over and see the cave one day and found it disappointing, but the ride was nice and the view was great so we felt we'd gotten our $1 worth. The cave is located on the shore side of the airport, at the end where planes land. Look for the road that goes by the edge of the sea and follow that to the second dirt road off to the right. Go down the dirt road and you'll find a small hand-painted sign saying Crusoe's Cave. That's the Crooks' house you'll see. Just give a shout and Mrs. Crooks or her daughter will collect your $1 and point you in the right direction.

Grafton Estate Bird Sanctuary, Black Rock

This is a small bird sanctuary and the site of the restored Grafton Estate House.

Hillsborough Dam

Take a left from Windward Road, at the sign between Mt. St. George and Granby Point.

This is an interesting stop for nature lovers and birdwatchers. Although we were not so lucky, friends spotted small caiman.

King's Bay Waterfall, Delaford

One hundred feet high and running well in rainy season, this is one more reason to explore this part of the island. Don't miss King's Bay Beach while you're in the area.

Main Ridge Forest Reserve

Bloody Bay Road, between Roxborough and Bloody Bay
on the eastern end of the island.

Protected since 1765, this rainforest lies at the eastern end of the island at an altitude of 2,000 feet, between **Roxborough** on the Atlantic coast and **Parlatuvier** on the Caribbean side. There is an excellent road crossing the island between these towns and at mid-point along this road you'll see signs for the forest. Help yourself to its treasures; a guide is not necessary. The preserve is large and it's a wonderful walk. We went in as far as the Gold Coin Waterfall, so named because the rocks have turned golden where the water rushes over them, but you can continue for hours.

Mystery Tombstone, Plymouth

If you are passing through Plymouth, do stop and take a look at this historical oddity. You'll find a small gravestone with the following inscription "She was a mother without knowing it and a wife without letting her husband know it except by her kind indulgences to him" – Betty Stiven 1783.

Parlatuvier Bay

This is a small exquisite bay and it was my favorite on the island until a concrete fishing pier was constructed in the middle. There is a small village. The beach is shaded by palms and the surf is gentle. A photograph from the hill overlooking the bay was a must before the pier was built.

Richmond Great House

Belle Garden, ☎ *660-4467*

This is a restored plantation house set in the hills. It is now an inn with a good restaurant. It has wonderful views and is an ideal spot for a relaxing lunch. Make a reservation the day before you go. Hiking on any one of the trails through the hills nearby will help you work off lunch.

Birdwatching

While Tobago does not have the variety of birds you may see in Trinidad, it does offer easier observation. **Roxborough** in the afternoon is a great place to see whole flocks of parrots flying from tree to tree. **Little Tobago** is a favorite; the **Grafton Estate Bird Sanctuary, Hillsborough Dam, St. Giles Island** and the **rainforest** are good too. Tobago has lots of trails to explore.

Beaches

Tobago has a wealth of beaches and many have public baths, changing rooms, and bar/restaurants. No beach is crowded and many are romantic and private. Generally, the more desirable beaches are on the Caribbean side of the island, where the water is calmer. This works out well as the Atlantic side of the island is more populated with small towns.

Bacolet Beach

There was no one on this isolated beach the day we were there. In the 60's, the Beatles are said to have frolicked here and, with all the choices they must have had at the time, they made a good one. Bacolet was also used to film scenes for the movie *Swiss Family Robinson*. The sand is tannish-gray as on many of the island's beaches and the surf is not too rough.

Buccoo Beach

With very calm water and gray, well-packed sand, this is a narrow beach that curves out to the point of the bay, giving lots of space to wander off for private sunning or swimming. Recently, there has been serious erosion in front of the beach facilities. Further away there is still a narrow strip of sandy beach to explore. There are changing rooms and a bar.

On Sunday evening there's a raucous "Sunday School" right on the beach, with music and dancing and general revelry. There is no food available at the beach itself, but there are lots of small mom and pop's nearby where you can try some local cuisine. La Tartaruga is about 100 feet from the beach, if you're looking for finer fare. It's open only in the evenings, but never on Sunday or Monday.

Englishman's Bay

Just east of Castara

One of the prettiest bays on the island. Although it's scheduled for development, right now it's lovely and there's nothing to get between you and the blue Caribbean sea. The sand is course tan and the waves are just right for swimming and snorkeling. Some days there are thousands of tiny fish circling so closely they look like one big rock or coral bed, but if you heave a stone in the water close by you can see the "rock" dissolve and reform itself. There are lots of gommangalala lizards on the trees and a lovely lady named Maureen sells great potato pies and coconut cakes. We had a delicious lunch for $4. There are no changing facilities, but lots of places to do a quick change in relative privacy. If you're not a sun worshipper, I'd especially recommend going in the late afternoon, say after 4 PM. You can have the beach all to yourself and see a lovely sunset with very romantic possibilities.

Grafton Beach, Stone Haven Bay

Grafton is one of the prettiest beaches in Tobago. Lined with tall palms, it typifies the Caribbean. The surf is light, so this is an excellent spot for swimming and sunning. The sand is a pretty tan and, although there are some small stones here and there, it's a good beach for walking. Though this beach is used by major resort hotels, such as the Grafton just across the road, you won't find it crowded. If you're not comfortable with isolated spots this is perfect. There are no public changing facilities, but there is a nice bar and beach food restaurant called the Buccaneer. It's owned and operated by the Grafton Hotel. Just across the road is the Sea Horse Inn, a lovely new bar/restaurant.

King's, Delaford

With deep grey sand, a pebbly bottom, and surrounded by thick vegetation, this is an out-of-the-way beach with lots of privacy and few tourists. Located in Delaford, King's Bay is an Atlantic Ocean beach, but the water is calm and luring. There are changing rooms and picnic tables. If you're there in the afternoon, you can buy fresh caught fish right on the beach.

Charlotteville

Man-o-War Bay

In Charlotteville, one of the more picturesque villages in Tobago, Man-o-War Bay is a sheltered harbor at this end of the island. The water is calm and good for swimming. The village is nearby.

Pirate's Bay Beach

Just around the corner and over the hill from Man-o-War Bay, this is a delightful private setting used by locals and visitors to Charlottesville. Yachts occasionally anchor off here, too.

Mt. Irvine Bay Beach

Just down the road from the Mt. Irvine Hotel, the beach has a small bar/restaurant owned by the hotel and operated for its guests and the public. There is also a watersports shop that can provide whatever you'll need in the way of equipment while on the island. Mt. Irvine Beach has hotel facilities at one end and the public facilities at the other. It's a toss up as to who gets the better end. There are changing facilities and baths along with a beach-side bar/restaurant and picnic sites, all nestled under tall palms. The beach itself is long and relatively narrow with tan sand and a comfortable surf. The beach facilities here are very attractive and I think the best on the island, with the possible exception of Pigeon Point.

Crown Point

Pigeon Point Beach Resort

Open from 8 AM to 6 PM, it is the only beach on the island with an entrance fee. For $1.75 per person you get your money's worth – calm aqua waters, palm trees and gardens, and soft white sand. Offshore lies Buccoo Reef. There are changing facilities, bathrooms, and small restaurants. You may hear or read that it's a populated beach, but by US standards it's empty and very beautiful. This is the sort of place you can settle into for the whole day, day after day. Sailfish are for rent and there are small craft and gift shops just before the entrance.

Store Bay Beach

This is the most popular beach on the island, according to locals. This doesn't mean that it's a busy beach by US standards though. The water is an azure-blue and the surf can range from very calm to active. Store Bay is a great swimming beach and good for socializing both in and out of the water. You'll see parents and children frolicking in the ocean after a hot day at work and school. It's a great place to talk with locals. Just up from the beach are vendors selling island crafts and several of the tiniest restaurants you'll ever see. These include Miss Jean's and Miss Esmie's, where the food is simple, but very good. Try the *roti*.

Store Bay

Sports

Tobago is a quiet island and, with few exceptions, activities are focused on the sea. Above and below the water you'll have every chance to explore this small wonder. Listed below are some of the sports available to you. In almost all cases, experts or novices will fit in somewhere.

Boat Charters

Boat charters to Buccoo Reef, Coral Garden, Nylon Pool and the Mangroves, with snorkeling equipment and soft drinks provided, cost as follows: two persons $90; four persons $105; and six persons $122. See Mt. Irvine Bay Beach, under *Beaches*, above.

Diving

Diving on Tobago is primarily for those with experience. The waters are not as clear as in other areas of the Caribbean, but diving challenges and opportunities to see large species are plentiful. Most divers spend their time in **Speyside**, where the reef is undamaged and larger fish and rays abound. Depths range from 70 to 90 feet in that area. For less experienced divers, **Buccoo Reef** offers many smaller fish and the wonderful coral gardens.

Diving is taken seriously on the island and the risks are respected appropriately. Dive masters will want to see certification papers and dive logs, but will not lend them much credence until they've actually seen you dive. Be prepared for a cautious first experience. There are many dive shops on the island and the **Speyside Dive Shop** is a good one to consider. Before signing on with someone, check the quality of their equipment and boat, taking note of how well they've been maintained. Robin, a good friend of ours from England and an avid diver, especially liked **Tobago Dive Masters** in Speyside. He's a confirmed vegetarian and animal rights person and he loved the fact that Tobago Dive Masters didn't have a caged parrot or tied up monkey outside their shop. As divers, he found them very respectful of the sport and of the animals and plants they encountered underwater. They are not affiliated with a hotel and no advance arrangements are necessary. One disadvantage is that they don't have their own boat. Kevin Frank and Ellis John own the shop and are careful that each group of four divers has a separate dive master.

With varying depths and visibility you can expect to see mantas, nurse sharks, moray eels, lobsters nestled in the coral and conch.

Golf

There is one high-quality golf course on the island at the **Mt. Irvine Hotel**. Home to a pro-am tournament, it is an 18-hole, 6,500-yard course designed by the late John Harris. Greens fees for 18 holes will be $40; golf cart rentals are $30; club rentals $15; and caddy fees $10. All prices are quoted for 18 holes and all are subject to tax.

Kayaks

Kayaks are available at **Arnos Vale**, and **Grafton Beach** hotels, and at **Watersports**, Mt. Irvine Bay Beach. Rental charges will be about $35 per day (less for a partial day).

Sailfish

Available for rent at **Pigeon Point.**

Snorkeling

Buccoo Reef is fantastic, but good spots can be found all over the island. **Arnos Vale** is especially good. Although the hotel looks very private, you'll have no problem using the beach. You can rent equipment in lots of places, but serious snorkelers should bring their own.

Sport Fishing

See **Watersports** at Mt. Irvine Bay. On the 32-foot pirogue *Super Star,* with twin 100 hp outboards, you can fish for marlin, tuna, mahi mahi, wahoo, kingfish, and barracuda. Light drinks and sandwiches are included in the price of $250 for a half-day and $395 for a whole day. You can also comfortably talk to any of the fishermen you'll see on the beaches and many of them will be happy to take you out.

Tennis

The **Grafton, Mt. Irvine, Coco Reef, Turtle Beach, Speyside,** and **Crown Point Beach** hotels all have asphalt courts. Hotel guests have free access during the day, but pay small fees for lights in the evening. The Crown Point courts are not in great condition and their lighting system is currently under repair. There are public courts in **Scarborough** open and lit till 11 PM.

Waterskiing

Waterskiing is not very common on the island, but you can give it a try at **Watersports** on Mt. Irvine Bay Beach.

Windsurfing

You can rent equipment at **Watersports**, Mt. Irvine Bay Beach, and at **Pigeon Point Beach Club** in Crown Point. The price will be under $50 per day or $25 for half a day.

A Day's Drive

This section is for those of you who, like us, don't have a good sense of direction. It always takes us a lot of time to figure out where we're going and how to get there again the next time we want to go. We hope this helps.

Scarborough/Bacolet

If you are on the southeast side of the island near Scarborough, make your way through Scarborough to Bacolet Street. It's not a long drive, but it is a nice one, passing some of the older homes on the island and offering a lovely ocean view most of the way. On this road you'll find **The Cotton House** clothing store, **Rouselle's restaurant**, and the **Old Donkey Cart Inn and Restaurant**. The latter two are great for dining, but only the Donkey Cart is open for lunch.

Just before Bacolet St. ends at Windward Road, you'll see an area on your right with a lot of older summer homes. These substantial homes are very sturdy and seem built for a much less hospitable climate.

Bacolet used to be *the* place to stay in Tobago, but its popularity declined since the airport was built in Crown Point. The area is lovely and well worth seeing. It's also a good region for budget travelers since you'll find more small guest houses here than in other rural areas.

Scarborough Market

Crown Point through Scarborough to Speyside & Charlotteville

If you're driving from Crown Point toward Scarborough on Milford Road, here is what you'll see: after passing through **Bon Accord** and **Canaan**, you'll come to **Canoe Bay** on your right (see *Camping*), then **Hampden Lowlands, Little Rockly Bay** (Palm Tree Village hotel), **Lambeau**, and, finally, **Scarborough**. Take a right at the sign for lower Scarborough and it will bring you into the center of town. Once you see the water, turn right.

Back up to the highway and turning right on the Windward Road, travel for about 1½ hours all the way to the other end of the island – Speyside and Charlotteville. It's a relatively narrow and twisted road, but it has some great ocean views and will take you through several small villages. On this road, you'll find the entrance to **Argyle Waterfall**, the **Richmond Great House**, and **Roxborough**, a great town for birdwatching in the morning or early evening. Roxborough is also home of an the old cocoa estate.

In Roxborough you have the choice of continuing on toward Speyside or taking the new road across the island toward Parlatuvier. If you take the cross-island road, about midway along you'll find the **Main Ridge Forest Reserve**. This is one of the few roads on the island that is in perfect condition and there is little or no traffic.

Crown Point & The Caribbean Side Of Tobago

If you want to explore the Caribbean side of the island, leave Crown Point on Milford Road. Pass through Bon Accord and Canaan, where you'll find the Penny Savers Supermarket, Peacock Mill Inn, and Golden Grove Farm. Take a left at Shirvan Road and you'll see the Starting Gate Pub on your right and then a sign for Moshead's store.

Plymouth coastline

After passing the sign for Mt. Pleasant on the right, take a left at the sign for Buccoo and follow it down to **Buccoo Beach**. There you'll find the Buccoo Beach Facility. Restaurants, such as **La Tartaruga**, are right by the beach and there are lots of smaller places; try the **Teaside Pizzeria**, **Hendrix Sandwich Bar**, and the **Match box**. You can rent bikes or visit on Sunday evenings for Sunday School.

Return to the main road (Shirvan) and turn to the left. You'll pass Mt. Irvine Bay Hotel on the right, Mt. Irvine Bay Beach and the watersports shop on the left. Not much further along the road, take a left at the sign for Stone Haven Bay. You'll see the back of the Grafton Hotel, Grafton Beach, the Sea Horse Inn, and Buccaneers Bar. Return to the main road and pass by the new Le Grand Courland Hotel and, next door, the Grafton Hotel.

Take a left at the sign for Black Rock and an immediate right. Follow it to the end and you'll find yourself at Turtle Beach. Return to the main road and turn left. Continuing, you'll pass the **Black Rock Café** and the **Turtle Beach Hotel**. Just past the Turtle Beach Hotel, turn left over Courland Bridge. Follow the road into Plymouth, where you'll find the **mystery tombstone** and **Ft. James**. Plymouth is a quiet small town without too much charm. Turn around and head back.

Tobago Daytrips

Old-style house, Plymouth

Take a left at Arnos Vale Road, where you'll find the **Arnos Vale Hotel**, a great spot for snorkeling. Arnos Vale is a very hilly part of the island. Driving past the hotel, you'll find a dirt road leading up a hill. Up ahead on the left you'll see a small wooden house owned by an older American fellow. Although we missed him each time we were there, he's said to be very willing to share his knowledge of the island. The views from just in front of his tiny house are fantastic. Just there you'll see a small paved road to the right. It leads up to a private home called Mot Mot Ridge, listed in the rental section.

Drive back down by the Arnos Vale Hotel and turn left. You can follow this road through hills and villages to arrive at **Englishman's Bay** and **Parlatuvier**.

Tobago's roads are not in great condition and signs are sometimes absent or misleading. Not to worry. There just aren't that many wrong turns to make and everyone is friendly and helpful if you get lost.

Shopping

Shopping does not even make it onto my list of things to do in Tobago. You'll run into opportunities to buy crafts, handmade jewelry, sandals, and clothes in various spots on the island, and if you need to bring back souvenirs, you are sure to find something acceptable, but that's about it.

At **Store Bay** and at the entrance to **Pigeon Point Beach** there are small stalls selling this and that. At the airport you can buy local candies made with sesame seeds and nuts, which are quite tasty. There are also a few shops at the airport selling sun lotions, over-the-counter cure alls, and tourist gifts. Hotel gift shops are not any more interesting and prices are very high for what's offered. Opportunities for parting with a few dollars are improving as more hotels open – try the shops at **The Grand Courland**.

Byran, local craftsperson

One interesting development for the devoted shopper is the little crafts and clothing stalls popping up along the Windward road to Speyside. Obviously, people feel they have something to offer and that's a good beginning.

The Cotton House on Old Windward Road in Bacolet will pass for a real shopping opportunity. They make lots of comfortable colorful Caribbean-style clothing in bright batik colors. The clothes didn't have the great feel of cotton I look for, though, and prices seemed a little on the high side.

Tour Guides

With the exception of excellent scuba diving and snorkeling services, Tobago needs to work on the quality and pricing of its guided tours. There is much to see on the island and much to learn, but we did not find the well-informed guides we have found in other countries. In general, they don't seem very knowledgeable about local plants, animals or birds.

Guided tours are a little expensive for what you get, but when first in Tobago you might find it worthwhile to hire a driver for a circuit

Tobago Tours

of the island. It's a good way to get oriented and have a sense of what you'd like to explore further. Later, you can rent a car and take off on your own. Remember, Tobago is safe and it's hard to go wrong, even if you get terribly lost. The island is not so big that you can't find your way around and there's always someone by the side of the road to point you in the right direction. Here is a list of available tour services by category.

Diving & Snorkeling

AquaMarine Dive, Ltd., Blue Waters Inn, Speyside (mailing address: P.O. Box 402, Scarborough). ☎ 660-4341 or Fax 639-4416. Snorkeling and scuba diving services are available for everyone, from very experienced to novice divers. PADI certification courses are offered beginning at $375, which includes four dives. Specialized advanced courses, such as search and recovery, are also taught. Rental equipment is available.

Dive Tobago, Ltd., Pigeon Point, Crown Point, ☎ 639-0202. Right next to the Conrado Hotel, Dive Tobago will give you a three-hour resort course for $55. It includes 1½ hours of instruction by the shore and another 1½-hour trip to a nearby reef, where you will dive with a fully trained diver. You'll not be left alone. This is a wonderful way to discover if scuba diving is for you. Each person is taught individually and they'll even give you a certificate saying you've completed a resort course. This course came highly recommended by an English friend, Frank Reese. He had always wanted to try diving and found that he loved it. Frank learned how to clear his mask, work with weights, how to use hand signals and his instructor never left his side, which he found very reassuring.

Man Friday Diving, Charlotteville, ☎/Fax 660-4676.

Tobago Dive Masters, P.O. Box 351, Scarborough, ☎ 639-4347 or Fax 639-4180. Ellis John, owner and manager, has his dive shop in Speyside. They offer PADI certification, glass bottom boat rides, and transportation to and from all hotels

Tobago Dive Experience has two locations: The Grafton Hotel, Black Rock, ☎ 639-0191 and Fax 639-0030; or The Manta Lodge, Speyside, ☎ 660-5268 or Fax 660-5030. This is a full-service dive company offering PADI and NAUI certification and advanced courses. They have equipment rentals and offer various dive packages.

Fishing

Dillon's Fishing Charter, Pigeon Point, ☎ 639-8765 or 639-2938. On his 38' Bertram sport fisherman, Dillon will take you for a full or half-day of fishing in the waters off Tobago. Fish are plentiful and it's unlikely they'll all get away.

Full-day charters are $400 and give you an opportunity for blue marlin, sail fish, wahoo, and tuna. Half-day charters are $250, with expected catches of dolphin fish, king fish, and barracudas. The charter is for a maximum of six persons.

Hard Play, Friendship Estate, Canaan, ☎ 639-7108. Go to sea with Captain Gerard "Frothy" De Silva in search of fish. Full-day charters are $400 and give you an opportunity for blue marlin, sail fish, wahoo, and tuna. Half-day charters are $250, with expected catches of dolphin fish, king fish, and barracudas. The charter is for a maximum of six persons.

Lincoln Yates

For the truly seaworthy, who would like to experience fishing 20 to 25 miles out in a 25-ft. launch, just talk to any fisherman at Pigeon Point or ask there for Lincoln Yates. He can tell you who to talk with.

Tobago Tours

Watersports

Watersports, Mt. Irvine Bay Beach, ☎ 639-9379 day or 639-9379 evenings.

Owner Bertrand Bhikarry will fix you up with everything you'll need for snorkeling, kayaking, waterskiing, windsurfing, surfing, boat and fishing charters. This is the only complete watersports facility on the island. You won't find jet skis though; Bertrand is committed to preserving the island's idyllic nature. They take credit cards or cash and are open to negotiating on prices for groups or multiple rentals. Take a moment to read Bertrand's essay on pulling a seine on page 144

Land Tours

Hoskin Antoine, 44 Sangsters Hill, Scarborough, ☎ 639-4138. Hoskin specializes in small groups up to eight persons. He's a good man for a day's tour of the island. Hoskin is interesting, reliable, and a very congenial person to spend time with.

Land Tours for Birders

David Rooks Nature Tours, Scarborough, ☎/Fax 639-3325 or 639-4276. An older German resident, David leads a variety of land tours, including the rainforest and Little Tobago. Make sure he'll be leading the tour you sign up for.

Yachting

This section of our guide is written for the yachtsperson. It was not an anticipated chapter when we planned the book. Both of us have seen boat yards in the UK, Barcelona, Palma de Majorca, Portugal, the US and the Caribbean. On our visit here we had an opportunity to look over the yacht facilities and were so favorably impressed by the services and prices on offer, we decided to add this chapter.

A Growing Industry

Until very recently, T & T was not a popular Caribbean destination for the sailing crowd. It is the most southerly of the Caribbean countries and its attractions were not widely known. In 1995, with the extreme season of hurricanes, Trinidad found itself home to hundreds of yachts seeking shelter. Once there, yacht owners discovered not only the delights of visiting T & T, but also found a marvelous resource for boat repair, maintenance, and storage. Suddenly T & T's southerly location – out of the active Caribbean hurricane zone – became a major advantage.

In 1990 there were only a handful of non-local yachts in the Chaguaramas harbors and storage facilities in the northwestern corner of Trinidad. By 1995 that number had grown to 2,500. Most of these yachts are in storage or undergoing repairs. There are a variety of anchoring and mooring areas and none are overcrowded.

More yachts are expected in the future. To assist in welcoming arrivals, the *Trinidad and Tobago Boater's Guide,* published by Jack Dausend, is being distributed at marine centers free of charge. It is a directory of available services and provides summary information on marinas and boat repair yards in the Chaguaramas area.

Chaguaramas has six marinas/boatyards. The allure for the yacht traveler became readily apparent after the 1995 hurricane season. We were surprised to find hauling-out facilities that managed very small boats along with those weighing 175 tons or more. This, coupled with their expert shipwrights, sailmakers, mechanics, and painters, means that T & T has full-service facilities. The quality of skills, labor, and the professionalism found here will please you, especially by comparison to work done in other, better-known yachting countries. Insurance, which in other areas may have been prohibitively expensive, may now be affordable, thanks to Trinidad's very favorable location. Your intended month stay-over for minor repairs might easily turn into a total overhaul or refurbishing, especially when you could save 50% over other countries in labor alone.

Professionalism abounds in yard foremen. The skill of the tradesmen and laborers and the wealth of top-notch equipment they work with will ensure quality work and will make your stay very productive.

Yachts at Chaguaramas

The T & T Advantage

Range Of Yards

The five existing yards with haul-out services, and the new Crews Inn coming on line will offer you a range of choices to meet your specific needs. Yards range from full-service haul-out facilities to yards that offer a laid-back relaxed atmosphere where you can do the work yourself and contract out when need be. Wherever you end up, you will no doubt feel that you have found "the yard" for you.

Those who do not want to commit to using only the on-site contractors of a particular yard will find most yards are flexible in allowing you to hire outside contractors. They will even provide you with a list of accredited tradesman who will supply estimates and work with you independently. This can be a very appealing alternative, allowing you to hire those who will best meet your needs.

For services that may not be available at the yard you choose, such as special machining needs, you can contract with support industry in the area or in San Fernando for highly specialized machine work. (San Fernando is the heart of the oil and gas industry.) Yards in Trinidad can also supply quality materials, from stainless steel to locally grown teak. Good quality marine ply, however, could be a problem. For those who know how difficult an out-haul can be when you can't get machining or special materials for those unforseen repairs, Trinidad is a pleasure. Welding aluminum and stainless steel is second nature for Trinidad – their oil and gas industry has been around since 1910.

Boats in transit receive an added benefit – service is free of tax and VAT. Before you order and buy, verify your in-transit status with the chandlery to assure that you are not charged tax.

Thanks to our shrinking world, any special orders you may need can be shipped by FedEx, the best of the available carriers, from Miami or elsewhere in only four working days. You may find yourself settling in for some significant work, like a couple of our friends from Florida who sailed to Trinidad for a haul out. After finding prices so reasonable compared to their home base in the States, they had a container shipped from the States (VAT excluded, thanks to their in-transit status) and spent the better part of a year doing a complete overhaul.

Customs & Immigration

Your arrival will be facilitated thanks to T & T's private port facility at Chaguaramas Terminals, Ltd., ☎ 627-5680. In the past, customs and immigration had to be done in Port of Spain, along with commercial traffic.

Yachting

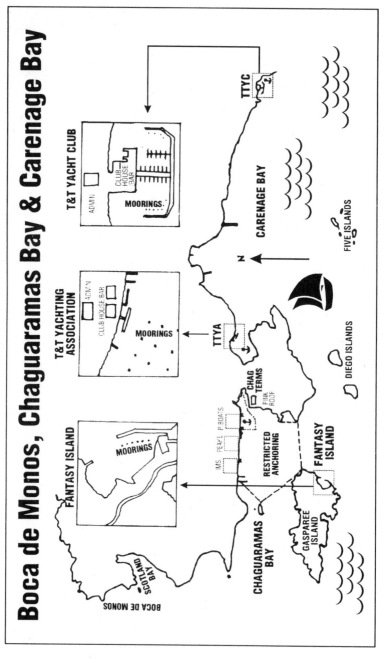

Map provided courtesy of the Trinidad and Tobago Boater's Guide –
1996; Jack Dausend, Publisher.

In Summary

Best of all is Trinidad's most valuable resource – its people. The yard foremen are knowledgeable, the tradesmen are professional, and the laborers friendly and receptive. These human advantages, coupled with the sophistication of the technical sector, will well-serve your yachting needs no matter the size of your vessel.

After your yacht's repairs are underway, don't forget to take in some of the sights of this richly beautiful and varied country. Trinidad alone is full of adventure, with a wide variety of things to see and do. Tobago might be considered for a vacation from the yacht. The 25-minute flight to the island is inexpensive and a few days stay would be a nice break. Tobago has no facilities for yachts, but anchoring off is allowed in some areas: Store Bay, Mount Irvine, Man-o-War Bay, and Courland Bay are a few of the favorites. Gas and water are available at Charlotteville on the extreme eastern end of the island.

The following is a listing of Trinidad's yachting facilities. All prices quoted are subject to change; please verify with the yard or service of interest to you.

Yachting

Directory of Yards

IMS Yacht Services, Chaguaramas Bay

Yard Manager, Chuck Jerningan
Yard Foreman, Kent Yohannson
P.O. Box 765
Port of Spain, Trinidad, W.I.
First Ave. South, Chaguaramas
☎ 625-2104/Fax 634-4437
Radio VHF channel 68

Facilities: Full-service haul out and storage facility, teak and wood shop, chandlery, fiberglass/osmosis repair, sandblasting, welding, corrosion protection, paint shop, sailmaker, office services, restaurant and bar, hot showers, security, laundry. They have a 70-ton Travelift.

Rates

Haul and Launch – 5 free days	$ 4-4.50/ft
Additional days on land (if working or living on board)	
6 to 21 days	$ .40/ft/day
22 to 90 days	$ .30/ft/day
91-plus days	$ .20/ft/day
Long term storage (no work being done)	
6 to 90 days	$ .18/ft/day
91-plus days	$ .15/ft/day
Chocking	
up to 50 tons or 60 feet	$20/boat
over 50 tons or 60 feet	$40/boat
Additional marine hoist time	$50/hour
Pressure washing	$ .65/ft

Note: There are discounts of 10% on advance payments of storage over six months.

Comments: This full-service yard is another fine complement to Trinidad's professionalism and service in the marine industries. Here you can take care of nearly all your needs on premises.

Peak Yacht Service, Chaguaramas Bay

Yard Manager, Franz Maingot/Yard Foreman, Augustus "Radix" Henry

Lot #5 Western Main Road, P.O. Box 3168 Carenage

Trinidad, West Indies

☎ 634-4427/Fax 634-4387

Radio VHF Channel 69

Facilities: Haul out and storage facility, marine grade services, 21 in-water berths, chandlery, welding, sandblasting, woodworking, fiberglass repair, painting, office services, water, electricity, fuel, laundry, showers, bar and restaurant, satellite TV, 10-room hotel with security. Their 150-ton Travelift allows up to 31 feet of beam.

Rates

Haul and launch up to 75 ft or 75 tons	$ 5/ft
(5 free days on land)	
Multihulls over 20 ft wide	$ 7.50/ft
Additional days on land (if working or living aboard)	
6 to 21 days	$ .50/ft/day
21 days to 3 months	$ .30/ft/day
3 months plus	$ .22/ft/day
Long-term storage (no work in progress)	
1 to 3 months	$ .18/ft/day
3 months plus	$ .15/ft/day
Multihulls – additional storage charges if over 20 feet wide.	
Chocking (stands and/or blocks)	
up to 60 feet or 50 tons	$20
up to 75 feet or 50 tons	$40
Greater than 75 feet	negotiable
Marine hoist time for special works	$ 1/ft
Pressure washing	$ .75/ft
Scraping	$ .45/ft
Cleanup	$ .30/ft
Use fee*	$20/month

*A temporary registration or membership fee for anchoring or mooring to use the facilities.)

Note: Discounts of up to 10% for advance payments on storage.

Comments: Peak Yacht Services prides itself on quality and professionalism. In this full-service yard, if you are contracting work to be done in your absence, you can probably sleep almost comfortably knowing the job will get done within specifications. Peak Yacht Services seems to run about as well as their air conditioners, which you'll see run just fine... Ah!

Power Boats Mutual Facilities Ltd., Chaguaramas Bay

Yard Foreman: Wayne Jackson
P.O. Box 3163, Carenage
Trinidad, West Indies
☎ 809-634-4303/Fax 809-634-4327
Radio VHF channel 72

Facilities: Haul-out and storage facility, 23 in-water berths, chandlery, welding, fiberglass repairs, woodworking, local teak, painting, office services, water/electricity, fuel, laundry, bar and restaurant, grocery, security, showers, and apartments. They have a 50-ton Acme.

Rates

Haul and launch (5 free days on land)	$ 4/ft
Additional days (if working or living aboard)	
less than 1 month	$ .40/ft/day
1 to 3 months	$ .30/ft/day
3 months plus	$ .20/ft/day
Storage (no work in progress)	
1 to 3 months	$ .18/ft/day
3-plus months	$ .15/ft/day
Chocking	$15/boat
Marine hoist time for special work	$50/hr
Pressure washing	$ .35/ft
Use fee*	$20/month

*A temporary registration or membership fee for anchoring or mooring to use the facilities.

Note: There are discounts for stays of three months or more, paid in advance.

Comment: Power Boats' main work is with sailing yachts. They give the personal and knowledgeable help you need regardless of the kind of boat you have. Power Boats backs contracted work 100%. For any job they will usually arrange at least three estimates for you. They charge a flat 10% of labor costs, for which they settle any disagreements or disputes. I doubt you will be anything but satisfied with this well-equipped and tightly-run yard. We heard nothing but compliments regarding the hands-on care and assistance. Wayne Jackson is getting quite a following of repeat satisfied customers.

Trinidad & Tobago Yachting Association (TTYA), Carenage Bay

Yard Manager: Claudette Jardine
P.O. Box 3140 Carenage
Trinidad, West Indies
☎/Fax 634-4376
Radio VHF Channel 68

Facilities: Full-service haul-out yard, moorings, repair shed, office services, water and electricity, laundry, bar and restaurant, security, and a good anchorage. They offer a 15-ton Travelift (max weight 30,000 lbs., max length 45 ft., max beam 15 ft.).

Rates

Haul and launch (7 free days on land)	$ 5/ft
Additional days on land (if working or living on board)	
8 to 21 days	$ .50/ft
21-plus days	$ .30/ft
Long-term storage (no work in progress)	
up to 3 months	$ .18/ft
3 months plus	$ .15/ft
Work in progress during storage or live aboard	$ .30/ft
Additional marine hoist time	$50/hr
Chocking	$20/boat
Engine or mast removal and replacement	$50
Mooring	$ 3/ft/month
Use fee	None

Comments: This is a private yacht club and school to teach sailing. Most boats anchor out. The anchorage is partially sheltered with a mud sand bottom. Approximate minimum draft is eight feet. Forty feet is pretty much the maximum boat size.

There is a capacity for approximately 50 foreign boats. Each boat owner sees about his own workers and workers tools. Arrangements can be made to use the on-premises work shed. This is a very laid back and fairly unhurried place. If you need odds and ends done and are comfortable doing the work yourself, this could be just the place for your smaller boat.

Yachting

Trinidad & Tobago Yacht Club, Carenage Bay next to Pt. Cumana

Club Manager: Mr. Power
Bayshore
Port of Spain, Trinidad, West Indies
☎/Fax: 637-4260
Radio VHF Channel 68

Facilities: There are 60 in-water berths, fuel dock (gas, diesel, water), laundry, showers, office services, security, bar and restaurant, and it's close to Port of Spain. This is a private club. As a foreigner, however, you can get a temporary membership. For each person on board your boat, you will pay approximately $10 per week or $25 per month to use the facilities.

Comment: This was the first yacht facility in Trinidad. There are slips for 45 boats with water and electricity, as well as hot showers. The slips are around $15/day or $260/month. The main advantage of the club is its proximity to Port of Spain. The anchorage is not as protected as you'll find in Chaguaramas, but it has a warm and friendly atmosphere. You will meet and greet a lot of travelers and it's a good stop for a happy hour get-together on Wednesdays and Fridays. Most people from Trinidad keep their boats here.

The Crews (Cruise) Inn, Point Gourde, Chaguaramas Bay

Boatyard & Port Operation Manager: Johan Van Druten
P.O. Box 518 Carenage
Trinidad, West Indies
☎ 634-4384/Fax 634-4542
Radio VHF channel 68

Facilities: Located next to T & T Customs in Chaguaramas Bay is the site of a most ambitious undertaking – Trinidad's first full-service marina, boat yard, shopping, and hotel complex. They are expected to have all these services in full operation by early 1997. On premises will be a 200-ton Travelift (32 ft. max. beam) as well as a 2.7-acre covered shipwright building and associated workshops. There will also be a grocery store, a marine supply shop, pharmacy, retail shops, a bank, and a restaurant/bar with entertainment.

Marina: The marina, open since mi- 1996, should be fully operational by winter. There are 63 slips, each supplied with water and electricity, cable TV, and telephone hookups. The marina will accommodate boats up to 100 feet. There will be a 900-foot commercial dock with water and fuel. Draft in the marina is 35 feet.

Comment: Johan Van Druten is doing everything possible to ensure the Crews Inn's success.

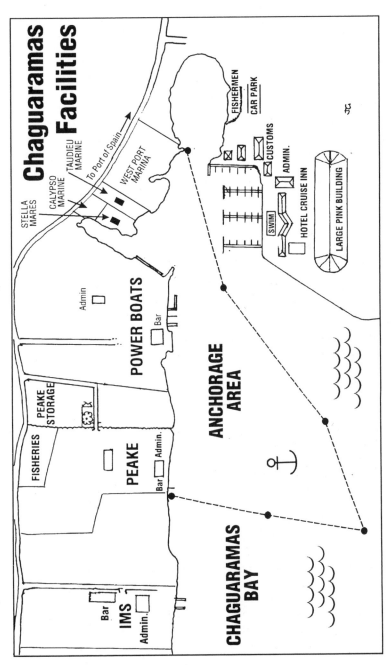

Map provided courtesy of the Trinidad and Tobago Boater's Guide –
1996; Jack Dausend, Publisher.

Eco-tourism & The Environment

Eco-tourism is an appealing phrase. It is the catch word for much of the tourism industry's advertising these days. Unfortunately, this does not mean that environmentally sound standards have been established or can be enforced. Even environmentally aware people are led into situations where the very land and ecosystems they want to protect are overburdened by the sheer number of visitors. But travel marketing is big business and words like eco-tourism sell travel programs.

People from more affluent regions sometimes look at developing countries and are outraged to see the lack of environmental controls, often forgetting that inexpensive goods produced there are products that we expect and use in our everyday lives. In eco-tourism, travelers want to get as close to the natural wonders of this world as they can. But in doing so, they often damage or destroy the natural world they come to see.

One of the concepts that should be central to eco-tourism is sustainability – carrying capacity. In other words, how many visitors can be accommodated while maintaining the quality of the experience for visitors and the quality of the environment for its native animals and plants. Pointe-à-Pierre in Trinidad has made the concept of carrying capacity a part of their overall educational program. They limit the number of visitors to the preserve so they may enjoy what is there without overwhelming the environment.

Trinidad and Tobago are beautiful. The natural environment offers a tremendous variety of vegetation and a wealth of animal life, both above and below the sea. The islands are extremely clean. Islanders often talked to us of their feelings about tourism and the problems it has created. Fishermen and divers complain about the consequences to their reefs. Tourists, often unknowingly, damage reefs by walking on them and by handling or breaking coral. Fishermen are dismayed when yachts anchor and drag their anchor chains on delicate reefs. Dumping waste near reefs has already caused over-fertilization and damage. Forest trails become less attractive when tourists absentmindedly break branches, pull leaves off plants, and pick wild flowers. Tourists put recyclable glass bottles in the trash. Although Coca Cola has a policy of non-reuse, most other bottles are recycled. One of our own observations might fit here as well. Appreciating the wonders of nature is best done with a clear head. Don't combine eco-tourism and alcohol.

Newsweek's issue of Feb. 5, 1996 had an article entitled "Beware of the Humans" and reported some of the abuses in eco-tourism. Go to your library and read this prior to your trip. Before signing on for one of these tours, ask probing questions about the expertise of the guides and about the controls that have been put in place to protect the environment.

Your Authors, Kathleen & Stassi

One at a time, please!

Bibliography

The British in the Caribbean, Cyril Hamshere, Harvard University Press, Cambridge, 1972.

A Continent of Islands, Searching for the Caribbean Destiny, Mark Kurlansky, Addison-Wesley Publishing Company, 1992.

A Short History of The West Indies, J.H. Parry and P.M. Sherlock, MacMillan St. Martin's Press, London, Third Edition, 1956.

History of the People of Trinidad and Tobago, Eric Williams, Andre Deutsch Limited, London, 1963.

Isles of the Caribbean, Special Publications Division, National Geographic Society, 1980, Robert L. Breeden, Editor, Special Publications Division. Call #972.9 Isles.

KAISO! The Trinidad Calypso, A Study of the Calypso as Oral Literature, Keith Q. Warner, Three Continents Press, Washington, D.C., 1985.

Callaloo, Calypso & Carnival, The Cuisines of Trinidad and Tobago, Dave Dewitt & Mary Jane Wilan, The Crossing Press, Freedom, CA, 1993.

Calypso Callaloo, Early Carnival Music in Trinidad, Donald R. Hill, University Press of Florida, Gainesville, FL, 1993.

Drawings of the Island's Past, Gerald G. Watterson, published by Gerald G. Watterson, St. James, Trinidad, 1993. This small book of drawings focusses on the old gingerbread homes and churches, many of which were destroyed by Hurricane Flora in 1963. Available at the Library in Scarborough, Tobago.

The Cruiser's Guide to Trinidad and Tobago, Norman Hover and George Glicksman.

The West Indies & The Guianas, D.A.G. Waddell, Prentice-Hall, Inc., Englewood Cliffs, NJ, 1967.

Please Note: Good books on Trinidad and Tobago's local animals and plants can be found at Asa Wright and Pointe-à-Pierre in Trinidad, as well as Man-o-War Bay Cottages in Charlotteville, Plantation Villas in Black Rock and at the Tobago Library in Scarborough, all in Tobago.

Index